Henry L. Lennard and
Leon J. Epstein
Arnold Bernstein
Donald C. Ransom

MYSTIFICATION AND DRUG MISUSE

❦❦❦❦❦❦❦❦❦❦❦❦❦❦❦❦❦❦

Hazards in Using Psychoactive Drugs

 Jossey-Bass Inc., Publishers
615 Montgomery Street • San Francisco • 1971

MYSTIFICATION AND DRUG MISUSE
Hazards in Using Psychoactive Agents
Henry L. Lennard, Leon J. Epstein,
Arnold Bernstein, and Donald C. Ransom

Jossey-Bass, Inc., Publishers
615 Montgomery Street
San Francisco, California 94111

Library of Congress Catalog Card Number 79-148657

International Standard Book Number ISBN 0-87589-091-1

Manufactured in the United States of America
Composed and printed by Hamilton Printing Company
Bound by Chas. H. Bohn & Co., Inc.
Jacket design by Daniel N. Talpers

HV
5801
• M9

FIRST EDITION

Code 7113

THE JOSSEY-BASS
BEHAVIORAL SCIENCE SERIES

General Editors

WILLIAM E. HENRY
University of Chicago

NEVITT SANFORD
Wright Institute, Berkeley

Preface

Last year, 202 million legal prescriptions for psychoactive drugs—stimulants, sedatives, tranquilizers, antidepressants—were filled in pharmacies for persons who saw their physicians first. During a time when the attention of both the public and most officials is concentrated upon the use of "illegal" drugs, this steady, marked increase in the giving and taking of legally prescribed or purchased psychoactive drugs has gone relatively unnoticed. From time to time warnings have been issued to the effect that the increased use of such drugs represents a very serious public health problem and that their continued misuse has very serious consequences. Such warnings have gone largely unheeded, and the prescribing and taking of psychoactive drugs have not abated.

Mystification and Drug Misuse deals with the mystification that surrounds the giving and taking of drugs, both legal and illegal, and describes how mystification, as practiced by the pharmaceutical industry, the medical profession, and the youth culture, contributes to the growing misuse and abuse of psychoactive drugs.

Preface

We consider all drug giving and drug taking within one broad conceptual framework because we believe that the issues attaching to the use and misuse of legal drugs are similar to those attaching to the use and misuse of illicit drugs.

Although most of the current voluminous writing about the misuse of drugs concerns the misuse of psychoactive agents by young people, and especially the use of drugs obtained illegally, we feel that to decry the use and misuse of drugs by young people while paying so little attention to the growing use and misuse of psychoactive agents in general, both those prescribed by physicians and those obtained over the counter without prescription, is highly misleading and unproductive. This broader perspective leads to conclusions about what social policies ought to be regarding the prevention of drug abuse which are very different from those implied by most of the current discussions about psychoactive drugs in medical journals and the mass media.

San Francisco
January 1971

HENRY L. LENNARD
LEON J. EPSTEIN
ARNOLD BERNSTEIN
DONALD C. RANSOM

Contents

Contents

"When the individual feels,
the community reels."

ALDOUS HUXLEY
Brave New World

The Risks and Problems
of Drug Misuse

うぐうぐうぐうぐうぐうぐうぐうぐうぐうぐう

In the giving and taking of drugs, one pays
for what one gets. The double entries in this ledger
are too often ignored and are too easily denied by
the youthful user of illegal drugs who thinks that
he gets something for nothing, who considers only
the immediate sensory experience, the ecstatic high
and freedom from anxiety, without attending to the
personal and group costs exacted. The inevitable
costs of drug use are also strenuously denied by
those advocates of "legal" drugs—physicians who
casually and consistently prescribe tranquilizers and
sedatives. Part of contemporary medical mythology
is that drugs somehow do not exact the same price
from the user when they are prescribed by a physician and that a patient can get relief from his
symptoms and escape from his troubles through
psychoactive drugs, providing they are duly prescribed.[1]

---

[1] We do not wish to minimize the considerable differences between legal and illegal drugs in terms of dose
standardization and purity of the chemical compound.

When physicians prescribe any drugs, they are or should be aware of the range of possible side effects. Under certain circumstances, with many drugs, the advantages may be clearly outweighed by the disadvantages. Penicillin, for example, causes allergic reactions in some and is fatal for a small number of patients. The use of penicillin in the presence of severe infections involving penicillin-sensitive microorganisms is not subject to question, but the use of penicillin for minor or nonspecific infections (which is unfortunately not a rare practice) is properly deplored by sophisticated physicians. The risks involved in such promiscuous drug use, especially when a drug of considerable potency is involved, are simply not outweighed by potential benefits. Furthermore, the issue becomes more complex when a drug known to have serious adverse side effects in a sizable number of patients (for example, Chloromycetin) is administered, because other treatments have failed. Here the danger to the patient is considerable because the infection is arrested.

Only when the effects of a drug are fairly well known can the value of using it be assessed in relation to its possible dangers and costs. Unfortunately, such knowledge is not available for most psychoactive drugs for two main reasons. First, psychoactive drugs have been used for only a comparatively short time. Second, their action tends to be less specific and more diffuse than that of other drugs in medical use. They not only alter body processes as do other drugs but also affect a whole complex of psychological and social processes connecting the individual with his physical and human environment. Thus,

2

these psychoactive agents, whether prescribed or self-administered, tend to elicit a broader range of unintended and unanticipated side effects, consequences, or costs than do other drugs. Sometimes the connection between such untoward consequences and the ingestion of a drug can be readily recognized. Sometimes the connection is not visible. Hidden costs tend to be ignored or denied both by those who administer and by those who take such drugs, especially if they have not themselves suffered untoward experiences. This denial of hidden costs commonly occurs with the use of illegal drugs.

Those in the medical profession or the youth culture who are inclined to deny or make light of the existence of such unanticipated and hidden consequences of psychoactive drugs may profitably ponder the unfortunate error of that most astute observer of human experience Sigmund Freud. As is well known, Freud was fascinated by the properties of cocaine and advocated its use for the treatment of psychological and nervous conditions. He did so on the basis of his own experience with the drug, and on that basis he considered it to be non-addictive and without serious side effects. As a matter of fact, Freud saw cocaine as most useful in the treatment of addictions and employed it in the treatment of the morphine addiction of his friend and colleague Ernst Fleischl-Marxow. Freud had to witness for many years to come the suffering which he had unwittingly induced in his close friend.

In letters to his financee, Martha Bernays,[2] Freud extolled the benefits of cocaine, which he took

[2] E. L. Freud (Ed.), *The Letters of Sigmund Freud* (New York: McGraw-Hill, 1960), pp. 195, 145.

before important social gatherings, to cure his migraine headaches, and to facilitate his writing. On January 20, 1886, Freud tells Martha of his visit to his teacher, the renowned psychiatrist under whom he was studying in Paris. "Charcot has reminded us once more of our appointment of Tuesday morning. . . . We drove there in a carriage. . . . R. was terribly nervous, I quite calm with the help of a small dose of cocaine, although his success was assured and I had reasons to fear making a blunder."

In another letter Freud writes:

I was suffering from migraine, the third attack this week, by the way, although I am otherwise in excellent health—I suspect the tartar sauce I had for lunch in Fleischl's room disagreed with me—I took some cocaine, watched the migraine vanish at once, went on writing my paper as well as a letter to Prof. Mendel, but I was so wound up that I had to go on working and writing and couldn't get to sleep before four in the morning. *Today I am in fine fettle again, very pleased with my paper, which is short but contains some very important information and should raise my esteem again in the eyes of the public.* [Emphasis ours.]

It does not appear from this letter that Freud recognized the possible connection between his use of cocaine and his being wound up or his inability to get to sleep until four. More serious, however, was Freud's extrapolating from his own experience with cocaine to advocate its use in psychiatric practice and to recommend its use to his friends and loved ones. He even asked his fiancee to take it.

Later and very painful experiences with giving the drug convinced Freud of his mistaken view of its harmlessness. Freud's enthusiastic advocacy of cocaine led one detractor to accuse him of having introduced the "third scourge of humanity." His biographer and friend Ernest Jones suggests that some of the subsequent antagonism to Freud's ideas on the sexual etiology of neurosis and other matters was related to this error of judgment with regard to the costs and benefits of cocaine.[3]

In later years Freud refused to use any drugs, even for the relief of pain, since he did not wish to experience the "clouding of consciousness" which he considered an inevitable accompaniment of sedative and analgesic medication. It may be well to keep this illustration in mind when confronted by the argument that it is after all the user of drugs who, on the basis of experience, is the best judge of drug effects and drug dangers. One should not simply disregard the judgment of a user as to the benefits and costs accruing from drug use. But since psychoactive drugs simultaneously affect a variety of physiological, psychological, and social functions, the answer to the question of recognizing and describing benefits and costs is too complex to be arrived at merely through individual subjective experience.

In addition to the judgment of the user, purely medical criteria are relevant. But so also are the personal and social values of the patient, his family, and community. For example, a physically

[3] *The Life and Work of Sigmund Freud,* Vol. 1 (New York: Basic Books, 1957), p. 85.

active patient may prefer to remain "anxious" rather than suffer the physical lethargy induced by a tranquilizing drug. A mature and creative individual may choose to take LSD in the hope of achieving a new synthesis, yet be aware of the potential risks involved in taking this hallucinogenic drug. What then is the justification for the medical profession's or the community's persuading or forcing one individual to take the drug and a second to abstain from its use? Perhaps disregard of individual options is justified when the individual may unwittingly endanger his own life or the lives of others in taking or failing to take a drug. But even here complex questions of value arise.

In 1387, six monks were imprisoned because they climbed Mount Pilatus, the highest mountain near Lucerne, Switzerland.[4] At the time such undertakings were viewed as a challenge to God or to demons. Not until the middle of the nineteenth century did mountain climbing become generally acceptable. Mountain climbing is now a respected activity, and men who risk their lives attempting new and dangerous ascents receive widespread sympathy and admiration. Particularly dangerous ascents take their yearly toll of the lives of mountaineers, yet each new dangerous exploration is greeted with admiration for the courage of the men who think they can succeed.

Many people who have taken hallucinogenic drugs argue that they too are explorers, that they are aware of the risk involved, but that the "trip" is worth the risk. Yet, society imposes severe legal sanc-

[4] V. Imseng, "Erstbesteigung des Sudlenz," 1870, in SAAS-FE Information 1970/71, Buchdruckerei, Visp A6.

6

tions on those who gamble their health or their lives in drug-taking, just as it once penalized those who wished to ascend high mountains. One must surely ask why it is considered so admirable to risk one's life climbing mountains while it is considered so reprehensible to risk it taking drugs.

Unfortunately, pioneers, those treading uncharted paths, are often caught unaware by new and unforeseen hazards. This is certainly true of those who pioneer in the discovery and use of new technologies. For instance, Wilhelm Roentgen the discoverer of X rays, could not fully recognize the untoward effects of continued exposure to X rays and many early workers died of overexposure. William Halsted, the first surgeon in the United States to use cocaine extensively as an anesthetic in surgery, became addicted to it as a result of using himself as a subject in his experiments with it.[5] Marie Curie similarly fell victim to radium poisoning.

> *She was working . . . with the singular imprudence which was usual with her. She had always scorned the precautions which she so severly imposed on her pupils. . . . Her blood content was abnormal. What of it? . . . For thirty-five years Mme. Curie had handled radium and breathed the emanation of radium.*

[5] Jones, *op. cit.* Vol. 1, p. 95: "In the same year, W. W. Halsted, America's greatest surgeon and one of the founders of modern surgery, injected [cocaine] into the nerves with success and thus laid the basis of nerve blocking for surgical purposes. He paid dearly, however, for his success, for he acquired a severe addiction to cocaine, and it took a long course of hospital treatment to free him from it. He was one of the first new drug addicts."

During the four years of the war she had been exposed to the even more dangerous radiation of the Roentgen apparatus. A slight deterioration in the blood, annoying and painful burns on the hands, which sometimes dried up and sometimes suppurated, were not, after all, such very severe punishments for the number of risks she had run! . . . Mme. Pierre Curie died at Sansellemoz on July 4, 1934. The disease was an aplastic pernicious anemia of rapid, feverish development. The bone marrow did not react, probably because it had been injured by a long accumulation of radiations.[6]

These examples bring to mind the fate of Timothy Leary, who pioneered in the investigation of hallucinogenic drugs such as LSD and psilocybin. Whatever history's final judgment of this complex man, it is clear that he made serious errors of judgment with regard to both the beneficial and the dangerous effects of these drugs. The ceaseless search which led him to ingest these drugs quite probably contributed to his rather extreme position on drugs and other matters.

When one sees young persons who have adventured along the drug route, clothed in rags, physically ill and mentally dulled, wandering the streets, they remind one of the victims and survivors of the Donner party, that group of intrepid pioneers who, unaware of the heavy snowfalls in the high Sierras, attempted to cross from Nevada to California. Without accurate knowledge of the weather,

[6] E. Curie, *Madame Curie*. (Garden City, N. Y.: Doubleday, 1938), p. 377.

8

the mountainous terrain, the means of protection against the heavy snowfall and hard winter, many members of the Donner party perished, while others paid a heavy physical price for their daring but ill-advised effort.

In the light of the range of costs exacted by all psychoactive agents, it is difficult to comprehend that the attention of both the public and most officials has centered upon the use of illegal drugs and that the steady, marked increase in the giving and taking of legally prescribed or purchased psychoactive drugs has gone relatively unnoticed. From time to time warnings have been issued to the effect that the increased use of such drugs represents a very serious public health problem and, in terms of cumulative consequences, that their abuse has very serious results. A former president of the American Academy of General Practice stated, "I have become deeply concerned about the use, overuse, and abuse of the psychic drugs—particularly the ones most commonly called tranquilizers. I believe these drugs are not only used wrongly, to excess, and without adequate indication but that in many instances their indiscriminate use has led to dependency, habituation, and addiction with all of the consequent results." [7]

Such warnings have gone largely unheeded, and the steady increase in the prescribing and taking of psychoactive drugs has not abated. These drugs

[7] C. Witten, address given to the American Academy of General Practice, in *Symposium: Non-Narcotic Drug Dependency and Addiction,* Proceedings of the New York County District Branch, American Psychiatric Association, March 10, 1966.

include energizers, so-called tranquilizers, psycho-
stimulants such as amphetamines, sedatives, and
hypnotics (both barbiturates and nonbarbiturates).
In 1969 pharmacists filled more than 202 million
prescriptions for such compounds, of which 80 million were new prescriptions (the rest were refills), in
a total population of 200 million people.[8] These fig-
ures would be substantially higher were they to include hospital and clinical usage. At the same that
prescriptions for legal drugs are on the increase, esti-
mates show the use of illegal drugs to be increasing
as well.

In whatever way this major scientific and social development will ultimately be appraised, the
introduction of psychoactive drugs into psychiatry,
into medical practice, and into the community at
large has generated a bewildering array of medical,
ethical, legal, and behavioral scientific questions—
questions of fact and theory—the implications of
which have not yet begun to receive the attention
they most surely deserve. Nor, indeed, has there ever
been a major effort to inventory the complex questions and issues involved.

We have elsewhere attempted to offer a comprehensive and general framework for thinking
about psychoactive drugs, their uses and effects.[9]
This book, however, deals with one of these significant areas, namely, the mystification that surrounds

[8] M. Balter, address given to the American Public
Health Association, Houston, October 1970.
[9] H. L. Lennard, L. J. Epstein, A. Bernstein, and
D. C. Ransom, *Drug Giving and Drug Taking: An Introduction to Sociopharmacology* (Chicago: University of Chicago Press, in preparation).

the giving and taking of drugs, both legal and illegal, and describes how mystification, as practiced by the pharmaceutical industry, the medical profession, and the youth culture contributes to the growing misuse and abuse of psychoactive drugs.

The process of mystification involves the definition of issues and situations in such a way as to obscure their most basic and important features. The way in which a situation is rendered may sometimes appear to be favorable to one party at another's party expense. However, the consequences of mystification often prove detrimental to all segments of a system. The act of mystification, by definition, tends to induce a mystified or confused state that is, however, not necessarily felt as such. The mystified party, while confused, may even view his mystifiers as benevolent and helpful.

The dangers of mystification reside in the fact that it is carried out implicitly rather than explicitly, making it harder to recognize the misleading construction of the situation. Whenever we detect mystification, we are alerted to the presence of a conflict that is being evaded or that is unrecognized by those involved. In this book we reveal some of the elements of the pervasive mystification that surrounds current psychoactive drug use and that in turn contributes to an ever increasing misuse of these drugs.

Drug abuse has traditionally referred to the physiological, psychological, and social problems associated with the illegal, excessive use of drugs for "nonmedical" purposes. The term *drug abuse* conjures up images of heroin addicts, traumatic withdrawal, pushers, and the underworld traffic in drugs with which these are connected. More recently, to these stereotypes have been added the colloquial descriptions *acid head* and *speed freak*. Problems associated with drug abuse have tended to be formulated in such terms as the recruitment of "susceptible" young persons into illegal drug use and the eventual physical and psychological deterioration if they persist in such use.

At the same time most of the research on psychoactive agents, their usefulness, and effect has been based on a symptom, disease, and treatment model. Information collected within this framework has been limited to an assessment of the effects of drugs on symptoms associated with emotional disturbance, and attention to other drug effects has generally focused upon troublesome physiological side effects. But attention clearly needs to be paid to other pervasive problems by studying the relation between drug usage and psychological, social, and interactional functions and patterns. This relationship includes the effects of drugs upon social groups and settings, considering effects on both the drugged and the nondrugged participants.

Before one can propose a program for the prevention of drug abuse, one needs to know about the functions drug giving and drug taking serve for physicians as well as for patients. We need to learn about the nature of the social settings and systems which encourage people to seek drug solutions for personal and social problems. We need to know whether the use of drugs furthers intimacy and relatedness among persons and satisfies their need for novel experiences or whether certain modes and functions of interaction are being sacrificed by their usc or whcthcr both results occur. More significantly still, we need to explore an uncharted territory regarding how the introduction of drugs into social systems affects the participants in these systems (families, hospital wards, neighborhoods, societies). For example, how many persons on what sorts of drugs bring about what sorts of changes in a social system as a whole? Certainly alterations of the psychological and social modes of behavior of a significant segment of a population can be expected to alter the population as a whole in significant respects.

In addition to the obvious types of drug abuse, the mere volume of increased drug use may also have dysfunctional side effects, leading to a subtle or secondary kind of drug abuse. In the same way that too many cars on the road results in an outcome opposite to that for which they were designed —to get us from place to place comfortably, safely, quickly—an extensive pattern of drug ingestion may undercut the very goals for which they were initially intended. Thus, the problem may not be so different from the one we now experience with the pollution of our earthly environment. The introduction and spread of psychoactive drugs in the human population may represent another kind of pollution, one which may also have the potential for precipitating an ecological catastrophe. An ecological model may indeed be relevant to an understanding of drug use and its consequences upon patterns of human interaction and the quality of human experience.

In this book we discuss the major segments of our society which are generating increased drug use. We first discuss the role of the pharmaceutical industry, which in the effort to expand its market of both presciption and nonprescription drugs has promoted its products by engaging in mystification. We then examine the role of the medical profession in drug misuse: the factors which encourage physicians' drug prescriptions and the considerations which make it likely for some patients to be given psychoactive drugs while others are not. The close relationship between the pharmaceutical industry and the medical profession receives our attention next. Both groups are interested in defining more and more problems as medical ones in order to justify both a medical model and the intervention with drugs. We show how the pharmaceutical industry, the mass media, physicians, and patients are wittingly or unwittingly locked in a vicious cycle of mutual mystification in which the problems of the human condition are increasingly medicalized. Mystification, however, is also prevalent in the youth culture. We suggest that young people often employ psychoactive drugs in ways and for purposes which are not dissimilar to those promulgated by the pharmaceutical industry and medical profession and which are analogous to the way in which many adults use alcohol.

Following the discussion of these major social elements is a treatment of the user as a judge of drug effects. We argue that misjudgment of the nature of drug action is common among users and present evidence for this point. A model explaining misjudgment of drug effects is presented.

Next we turn to costs and examine some consequences, visible and hidden, of excessive drug use. We raise the issue of side effects, both physical and social, and explore some larger dysfunctions of drug

14

taking. An examination of the models of drug action implicit in the use or, rather, misuse of psychoactive drugs then follows. We suggest an alternate, more appropriate model of drug action and the treatment of drug problems.

It is at this point that we deal with the larger societal matrix and discuss the effect of rapid social change on increased drug use. Finally, we conclude the book with recommendations to the medical profession, educators, and the public at large regarding social policies for the prevention of drug misuse. These recommendations follow from the conceptual framework developed in the book, a framework that includes a consideration of legal and illegal drugs, medical and nonmedical aspects of drug use, and the effects of drugs upon persons other than the user.

II

Mystification by the Pharmaceutical Industry

Pharmaceutical companies constitute an active industry which is constantly seeking a wider market for its products; and both physicians and the general public are targets for its detail men and intensive advertising campaigns. For drugs which require prescription, the industry believes it must educate physicians about their usefulness. Drug advertisements abound in medical journals and in many hospital lobbies. Scarcely a day passes in which a physician's mail does not include drug literature. Pierre Garai, a medical writer, states:

Tranquilizers have become a big business . . . a new national habit. . . . The physicians have been sold. So has the country. . . . Three quarters of a billion dollars are spent yearly by some sixty drug companies to reach, persuade, cajole, pamper, outwit, and sell one of America's smallest markets, the 180,000 physicians. . . . No other group in the country is so insistently sought after, chased, wooed, and downright importuned." [1]

Most pharmaceutical firms have experienced substantial growth since the early 1950s. For example, in 1951, one company reported net sales of 9.5 million dollars; by 1970, this sales figure had reached 83.6 million dollars.[2] Among the principal products of this company are central nervous stimulants (amphetamines and amphetamine-barbiturate combinations) and antipsychotic agents (phenothiazine compounds). While the sale of all drugs has increased greatly for the industry as a whole, the sale of psychoactive drugs has increased to a greater extent.

For nonprescription drugs, the industry advertises and sells directly to the public rather than to the physician, and this promotion they also accomplish with increasing success. From antacids to Compoz, there is a drug on the over-the-counter market for a remarkable variety of occasions. The proliferation of these drugs has become so great that the Federal Trade Commission has instituted an investigation of advertising practices and claims concerning their use.

The pharmaceutical industry alone can

[1] Quoted in S. Malitz, "Psychopharmacology: A Cultural Approach," in *Symposium: Non-Narcotic Drug Dependency and Addiction,* Proceedings of the New York County District Branch, American Psychiatric Association, March 10, 1966, p. 10.

[2] Standard and Poore's *Corporation Record,* 1951, 1970.

hardly be indicted for this inducement to increased drug usage. It is an American tradition that growth is good, and increased corporate earnings demand ever larger markets. If General Motors is to grow, it must convince American families they need two cars, not one, and the same logic holds for the pharmaceutical industry. We call attention to this factor mainly to suggest that steady pressures on the pharmaceutical industry induce it to encourage the use of drugs.

While the pharmaceutical industry has been expanding its market of both prescription and nonprescription drugs, it has in doing so created an increased need. It is in the construction of this need that the industry has promoted its products in part by engaging in what we feel can appropriately be called mystification. As we defined it in the previous chapter, this concept of mystification involves the communication of false and misleading explanations of events and experiences in place of accurate ones, explanations which serve one party at another party's expense.

In the context of current usage, drugs are medical agents whose function is the solution of medical problems. Only to the extent that interpersonal and other problems can be construed as medical-psychiatric problems can they be considered appropriate targets for drug treatment. As more and more facets of ordinary human conduct, interactions, and conflicts are considered to be medical problems, physicians and, subsequently, patients become convinced that intervention through the medium of psychoactive drugs is desirable or required.

The pharmaceutical industry is redefining

and relabeling as medical problems calling for drug intervention a wide range of human behaviors which, in the past, have been viewed as falling within the bounds of the normal trials and tribulations of human existence. Much evidence for this position is to be found in the advertisements of drug companies in medical journals, in direct mailings to physicians, and in advertising directed to the general public.

A series of examples illustrate this point. The first involves the personal conflict a young woman may experience when first going off to college. On the inside front cover of a professional journal [3] an advertisement states: "A whole new world . . . of anxiety. . . . To help free her of excessive anxiety . . . adjunctive Librium." Accompanying the bold print is a full-page picture of an attractive, worried-looking young woman, standing with an armful of books. In captions surrounding her, the potential problems of a new college student are foretold: "Exposure to new friends and other influences may force her to reevaluate herself and her goals. . . . Her newly stimulated intellectual curiosity may make her more sensitive to and apprehensive about unstable national and world conditions." The text suggests that Librium (chlordiazepoxide HCL), together with counseling and reassurance, "can help the anxious student to handle the primary problem and to 'get her back on her feet.' " Thus, the normal problems and conflicts associated with the status change and personal growth that accompany the college experience are relabeled as medical-psy-

[3] *Journal of the American College Health Association,* 1969, *17* (5).

chiatric problems and as such are subject to amelioration through Librium.

In another journal [4] an advertisement advises a physician how he can help deal with such everyday anxieties of childhood as school and dental visits. It portrays a tearful little girl, and in large type appear the words: "School, the dark, separation, dental visits, 'monsters'." On the subsequent page the physician is told in bold print that "the everyday anxieties of childhood sometimes get out of hand." In small print below he reads that "a child can usually deal with his anxieties. But sometimes the anxieties overpower the child. Then, he needs your help. . . . Your help may include Vistaril (hydroxyzine pamoate)." The advertisement, in effect, presents an oversimplified conception of behavior and behavior change. Potential anxiety engendered by new and different situations is defined as undesirable, as constituting a medical and psychiatric problem which requires the intervention of a physician and, most particularly, which requires intervention through the prescription of a psychoactive drug.

Physicians and parents with low tolerance for anxiety or those with limited ability to meet the demands of even a temporarily troubled child are those most likely to believe that the child is disturbed and in need of drug treatment. However, no substantial evidence supports the proposition that the prescribed drug does indeed facilitate children's participation in school situations. What is especially disturbing about advertisements such as

[4] *American Journal of Diseases of Children,* 1969, *118* (2).

this is that they tend to enlist the help of physicians in introducing children to a pattern of psychoactive drug use. Paradoxically, such drug use, at a later date, without a physician's prescription, is deplored both by the medical profession and by the community at large.

Finally, we come upon a box used to distribute samples of Tofranil (imipramine hydrochloride) to physicians.[5] On the box is a picture of an adolescent girl. Above the picture in bold print is the legend, "Missing, Kathy Miller." Below the picture we read, "$500 reward for information concerning her whereabouts." Alongside in white print we read the plea, "Kathy, please come home!" Inside the box is a letter entitled, "Kathy, We love you. . . . Please come home." We quote: "Dear Doctor: For parents, inability to communicate with their children is a significant loss. The 'What did I do wrong?' lament of the parent may be accompanied by feelings of incapacity, inferiority, guilt, and unworthiness. Many may, in fact, be suffering from symptoms of pathological depression. What can Tofranil, imipramine hydrochloride, do for your depressed patient?" There are multiple levels of mystification in this advertisement. First, it suggests that the problem of a runaway child is a medical or psychiatric problem, rather than a human or family problem to be viewed within the larger framework of conflicts between the outlooks and values of different generations. Furthermore the insert suggests that a parent's grief reaction in this situation is pathological rather than appropriate.

[5] Professional sample, Geigy Pharmaceutical, insert dated August 15, 1968.

And third, having placed the problem into the psychiatric realm, the advertisement recommends the use of the antidepressant Tofranil.

This advertisement is only one of many which, as R. C. Pillard pointed out in his testimony before a Congressional subcommittee,[6] imply that "antidepressant therapy is indicated in the griefs of everyday life" and which are "part of a trend to suggest the use both of antidepressants and tranquilizers not only for specific mental illness but to soothe life's ordinary woes." As was pointed out in testimony before Senator Gaylord Nelson's Congressional subcommittee [7] drug advertising has "taken on added significance to the medical profession in that for the most part there is no other compendium of drug information than the *Physician's Desk Reference*," which is composed of advertisements bought at the rate of $115 per column inch. "This book . . . [is] given away and . . . used by doctors as a source of objective information."

In his opening statement to the subcommittee hearings, Nelson [8] said, "There is growing concern . . . that the increasingly close financial relationship between the drug industry and the medical profession may be contrary to the best interests of the profession and the public." One result

[6] Statement before the Subcommittee on Monopoly of the Select Committee on Small Business, July 30, 1969 (Washington, D.C.: Government Printing Office, 1969), p. 5408.

[7] H. Brodkin, statement before the Subcommittee on Monopoly of Select Committee on Small Business, June 19, 1969. (Washington, D.C.: Government Printing Office, 1969), p. 5564.

[8] Opening Statement before the Subcommittee (*ibid.*), p. 5480.

of this relationship seems to be an increase in the prescription of all drugs. We are concerned that the contemporary trend of increasing prescription of psychoactive drugs is contributing to the recruitment of more and more persons into a way of life in which the regulation of personal and interpersonal processes is accomplished through the ingestion of drugs. Thus, when a physician prescribes a drug for the control or solution or both of personal problems of living, he does more than merely relieve the discomfort caused by the problem. He simultaneously communicates a model for an acceptable and useful way of dealing with personal and interpersonal problems. The implications attaching to this model and its long-term effects are what concern us.

III

Mystification by the Medical Profession

❧❧❧❧❧❧❧❧❧❧❧❧❧❧❧

When a physician prescribes drugs to a middle-aged woman who is upset about her child's rebellion or who is miserable in an unhappy marriage or to an elderly man or woman who has been isolated from children and community or to children who cause trouble in schools, he often only masks the problem. In these instances drugs serve to decrease the anxiety or unhappiness of the individual and, more importantly, thereby to decrease the amount of trouble his anxiety, misery, or unhappiness may be causing others. Drugs may thus make it possible for others to manage or to cope with the disturbed or disturbing individual.

The drugs do not, however, reach the sources of the anxiety or misery—sources which may reside, for example, in an unhappy marriage, in the unfortunate position of the elderly in our society, or in the unsuccessful socialization of many youngsters into group settings. In other words, drugs do not remedy the unfavorable social and interpersonal arrangements and personal circumstances which generate anxiety or unhappiness. Through the creation of chemical barriers and through the diminishment of gross social deviance, drugs may in fact perpetuate malignant patterns and social arrangements. Were drugs not so readily available, pressure for other solutions and the pursuit of alternative options might be encouraged.

The question as to where appropriate drug use ends and drug misuse begins is not easily answered. We suggest that drug abuse occurs when the costs of the latent fallout, or side effects, of the use of a drug outweigh its benefits (irrespective of whether these costs are reckoned in social, psychological, economic, or physiological terms) or when the benefits of drug use accrue more to the giver than to the taker.

The giving of drugs has always been and still remains the hallmark of the physician. This function not only has been assigned to him as part of his social role but for many drugs has been written into law as his exclusive prerogative. The giving of drugs by a physician is essential, if not intrinsic, to the practice of medicine. But at the same time the act of drug giving is a form of social behavior and as such entails social and psychological consequences that may transcend the purely medical purposes for which it is undertaken. Attention must therefore be paid to the latent (hidden) functions of the act of drug giving (and drug taking) as well as to the manifest (explicit) ones.

The manifest functions of a social process are, as R. K. Merton points out, "those objective consequences which are intended and recognized by participants in the system. Latent functions are those consequences neither intended nor recognized . . . . It is precisely the latent functions of a practice or belief which are *not* common knowledge." [1] The administration of a drug serves latent functions for physicians as well as for patients and for pushers as well as for addicts. Because these latent functions of drug giving go unrecognized and because they tend to promote drug giving for other than bona fide medical reasons, their operation tends to encourage drug abuse. Current medical practices in this area lead to two major latent consequences: benefits to the physician and further mystification in the use of drugs.

The availability of an effective drug legitimizes the physician-patient contract. Patients seen in everyday practice present physicians with complaints that are obviously troublesome to the patient and a source of concern for him. But often a physician can neither discover a specific cause for the patient's complaint nor clearly define the complaint for himself or for the patient. The physician nonetheless often prescribes medication. In such cases the drug prescribed is likely to be a minor tranquilizer to relieve the patient's discomfort. But such an action also serves latent functions. Prescribing a drug, such as a minor tranquilizer, legitimizes the doctor-patient relationship. Through giving a drug the physician accepts a patient's discomfort as legitimate, and he agrees with the patient's definition of himself as being sick. Through prescribing a drug, a physician also reduces a patient's anxiety by implying that he has defined the problem and can alleviate the complaint. This syndrome is clearly a form of mystification, albeit in a good cause.

[1] *Social Theory and Social Structure* (Rev. Ed.) (New York: Free Press, 1957), pp. 51, 68.

Despite the efforts of the mental health movement, considerable stigma still attaches in the community at large to psychiatric "illness." The administration of drugs for such conditions appears especially reassuring to individuals who still experience shame about mental illness and skepticism regarding psychotherapeutic procedures. The taking of a drug mobilizes an individual's expectancy of change and (in the case of hallucinogens) of having novel and valued experiences. As W. I. Thomas said some time ago, if individuals define situations as real, these situations *will be* real in their consequences. Most persons furthermore have learned to associate the administration and taking of drugs with the certainty, or at least the promise, of relief from illness, pain, or discomfort. Expectancies regarding the power of drugs are reinforced by the communication media through articles concerning the value of drugs and by the opinion leaders of the youth culture.

Prescribing a drug may also help a physician to maintain a sense of accomplishment and to allay his frustration. As studies of medical students suggest, physicians are likely to be most pleased by patients who permit them an opportunity to effectively apply their skills and knowledge. Physicians are likely to prefer to work with patients whose symptoms are definite and with whom, by applying their knowledge, they can facilitate healing.[2] The patients most physicians are likely to meet in gen-

[2] W. Martin, "Preferences for Types of Patients," in R. K. Merton, G. Reader, and P. L. Kendall (Eds.), *The Student Physician* (Cambridge, Mass.: Harvard University Press, 1957).

eral medical or psychiatric practice, however, do not always make this application of skills and knowledge possible. In the presence of an undefined and fluctuating symptomatology, a physician is less able to render the service he prefers and with which he is most comfortable and is less able to use his knowledge to the fullest. Because this situation is frustrating for the physician, the administration of a drug, even when based on the assumption of a partial placebo effect, may reduce his feeling of impotence.

Administration of drugs may help some physicians retain a sense of mastery in ambiguous situations, such as those associated with mental illnesses. The administration of potent antipsychotic agents may sometimes be credited to this phenomenon. Nothing is quite as frustrating for a psychiatrist or mental health professional as a seriously ill psychotic patient who does not respond to treatment. The readiness of some psychiatrists to use even new drugs, including some with incompletely determined hazards, may be testimony to a sense of such a perhaps unarticulated exasperation. And testimony can be found too in the suggestions of staff members that drug dosages be increased for patients who become agitated or disturb the routine of a ward.

A number of studies, to our mind, support some of the observations offered here. These suggest that prescribing a psychoactive drug helps a physician to preserve a sense of mastery in the doctor-patient relationship.

W. S. Appleton [3] studied the records of

[3] "Snow Phenomenon," *Psychiatry*, 1965, *28*, 88–93.

twenty-five patients who had been "snowed" with over 1500 mg of chlorpromazine per day. He found that the use of such large doses was correlated with the inexperience and anxiety of first-year residents; assaultive patients received massive doses most quickly with overactive destructive patients next. Appleton concluded (on the basis of the fact that none of the assaultive patients responded to massive dosages), "It is not surprising that psychiatric treatment taking place in an atmosphere of fear is not very successful."

Psychoactive drugs tend to be prescribed frequently by physicians who value being in control or who feel helpless in managing a patient or an interpersonal transaction without drugs. In this context M. Shabshin and M. B. Eisen [4] found that aggressiveness, not diagnostic category, seemed to determine who got medication and what kind. Using ward tension as a variable, they found that more patients were given drugs during weeks when ward tension was high. Other factors influencing drug administration were the ideology of the psychiatrist, the quantity and quality of available personnel, and economic factors such as size of units, number of patients per room, availability of recreational space, and how long the patient could stay in treatment.

Alternatives are available, however, in many situations. W. Mendell [5] reports that medical students, interns, and residents who participated in an

[4] "Effects of Ward Tension on the Quality and Quantity of Tranquilizer Utilization," *Annals of the New York Academy of Science,* 1957, *67,* 746–757.
[5] "Tranquilizer Prescribing as a Function of the Experience and Ability of the Therapist," *American Journal of Psychiatry,* 1967, *124* (1).

experiment in which the prescription of psychoactive drugs was not permitted for a patient during the first twelve hours of hospitalization tended to markedly decrease the number of prescriptions they wrote for patients in subsequent weeks on the service.

The number of drugs and the dosage levels prescribed vary considerably from institution to institution as well as within the same institution. This variation could well be attributed to differences in the severity of illnesses and in the clinical convictions of the staff members involved. But another interpretation can be advanced—namely, that the degree of tranquilization employed is related to characteristics of the social system or setting and the personality attributes of the personnel. For example, patients are most likely to be snowed with drugs in settings or systems which have the least tolerance for strain or deviance or in which external limitations (for example, limitations of staff and space) introduce constraints on the amount of strain or disturbance the system can tolerate.

Likewise, a family's request to a physician for higher drug dosage or a family's persistent reminders to a patient that he take his medication can be viewed either as an expression of concern for the patient's well-being or as an attempt to reduce friction or deviance within the family. We suggest that the most pressure for drug constraints occurs in families in which interaction processes are rigid and in which only a relatively narrow range of change can be accommodated and in families which show little tolerance for novelty.

Psychoactive drugs may also be used to reduce demand potential in a given context. When it is not possible to meet potential demands or when demands exceed the level of response which can be provided, drugs may serve to restrict demands and the need for a response. An example is the practice of providing sedatives for nighttime sleep to hospitalized patients. This practice, often unwelcome to the patients, is justified on the grounds that it gives the patient a good night's rest. But it is equally clear that while patients are asleep, the staff can turn their attention to other tasks which their jobs entail, without the added inconvenience of having to respond to demands from patients.

A publicized example of such overzealousness and mystification in the application of drugs to the solution of primarily nonmedical problems came to national attention in a report that between 5 and 10 per cent of the 62,000 school children in Omaha were being given behavior modification drugs (such as Ritalin, Tofranil, and Dexedrine).[6] The children, virtually all of them in grade school, were identified by their teachers as hyperactive and unmanageable. The school administration found itself swamped with the problems that grew out of the fact that so many elementary school children had potentially dangerous drugs in their pockets and in their lunch pails. "They were trading pills on the school grounds," the assistant school superintendent reported. "One kid would say, 'Here, you try my yellow one, and I'll try your pink one.' "

An Omaha pediatrician was instrumental in introducing the behavior modification program to

[6] *San Francisco Chronicle,* June 29, 1970, p. 1.

the public schools after he had attended a seminar in which he said several prominent physicians described the positive results they had achieved by using drugs on hyperactive students. Physicians thus introduced thousands of elementary school children to drugs which the United States Food and Drug Administration warns are addicting and which it urges physicians to exercise extreme caution in prescribing.

This example seems to us to be a paradigm of drug abuse by physicians and to exemplify the whole gamut of practices which must be reversed if such abuse is to be prevented: the use of drugs for social control; the use of drugs with dangerous or unknown side effects in the absence of a generally accepted need to do so in relation to serious illness; the induction of young persons into taking drugs as a way of solving problems; the substitution of a medical for a social model of influencing social behavior; the mystification of and by the physician as to the nature of the problem, the nature of drug action, and the description of drug effects.

To a much greater extent than is commonly assumed, whether or not a drug is prescribed for a patient, the kind of drug that is prescribed, and its dosage are not simply functions of the patient's symptoms or illness but depend frequently on characteristics of the physician. In other words, they depend more on whom the patient goes to see than on what brings the patient to seek help.

Psychoanalytically trained physicians, for instance, prescribe fewer psychoactive drugs than do other psychiatrists. Furthermore, they tend to prescribe "milder" drugs (such as Meprobamate, Librium, and Valium). It might be supposed that this difference occurs because psychoanalytic psychiatrists are less likely to encounter or to accept the kinds of patients who are treated by nonanalytic psychiatrists, but this is by no means always the case. In fact, one complaint lodged against dynamically oriented psychiatrists by those who advocate drug use is that they tend to treat with psychotherapy patients who should be treated with drugs.

More interesting still is that patients seen in increasing numbers by nonmedical therapists (whether they be analysts, psychologists, social workers, or group or family therapists) are likely to receive considerably less medication than do patients seen by physicians and psychiatrists. There is a considerable overlap in the patient populations seen by medical and nonmedical therapists. Who gets to see whom for treatment is more likely to be a function of time, space, money, and familiarity with the world of mental health than of diagnosis. Here again, then, drug prescription depends on whom the patient sees, not on his problem.

The social and personal characteristics of the physician also play an important role in determining the pattern of psychoactive drug prescription. A physician's age, for example, is an important factor in determining his pattern of prescription and his assessment of psychoactive agents.[7] Irrespective of psychiatric training, the younger the physician, the less he tends to utilize drugs and the less favorably he looks upon the effects of drug treatment. Age

[7] M. Hayman and R. Ditman, "Influence of Age and Orientation of Psychiatrists on Their Use of Drugs," *Comprehensive Psychiatry*, 1966, 7, 152–165.

difference in prescription patterns is in turn related to when medical and psychiatric training was obtained and the time elapsed since completion of professional training because a more cautious position in relation to the use all drugs, not only psychoactive drugs, is being adopted by the teaching faculties of medical schools. What a medical student, intern, or resident is taught about psychoactive drugs, their usefulness or limitations, obviously influences his prescription practices. Closely connected with what he is taught are his experiences with the use of psychoactive drugs during his training, as demonstrated in the ingenious study by Mendell already referred to.

Correlations between the frequency of psychoactive drug use and the personality of the prescriber have been demonstrated in a number of studies. We have already mentioned the correlation between drug prescriptions and a physicians need to feel in control of the doctor-patient relationship. In one study, psychiatric residents who scored high on an authoritarian personality measurement scale also ranked high in their use of drugs. The data of this study also suggest that "psychiatrists who use drug therapy frequently tend to value assertive and decisive behavior more than [do] their colleagues who use it to a lesser extent." [8]

Drug prescribing is also related to the social context within which medical practice is embedded. This context affects the frequency of psychoactive

[8] G. L. Klerman, M. R. Sharf, M. Holzman, and D. S. Levison, "Sociopsychological Characteristics of Resident Psychiatrists and Their Use of Drug Therapy," *American Journal of Psychiatry*, 1960, *117*.

drug use, the classes of drugs used, and the drug dosage level. In fact drug use varies very considerably from country to country. The average dosage of chlorpromazine, a drug designed for use with seriously disturbed persons, especially those diagnosed as schizophrenic, varies considerably among a number of European countries, ranging from a maximum average dosage of 300 mg per day in one country to 800 mg per day in another.[9]

Furthermore, drug giving by physicians varies depending on whether patients are treated in the physician's office, in a clinic, or in the ward. Moreover, characteristics of the community within which a physician practices—metropolitan, urban, or rural—and whether there is easy access to a university medical center apparently also affect patterns of prescription. A series of one hundred prescriptions written by residents practicing in a psychiatric outpatient service in a general hospital in a medium-sized city about 150 miles from San Francisco were compared with prescriptions written by psychiatric residents in the outpatient service of a psychiatric facility located in metropolitan San Francisco. Though the symptoms of the patients were similar, the differences in the types of psychoactive drugs prescribed were quite striking.[10] Differences were twofold. In both facilities there were prescriptions for similar drugs, though the specific drugs were not

[9] B. Wilkens and S. Malitz, "Some Problems of Dose Variation in the Use of the Tranquilizing Drugs," *American Journal of Psychiatry*, 1960, *117* (1), 23–29.

[10] H. L. Lennard and R. W. Brissenden, "Use of Psychoactive Agents in Two Outpatient Clinics," unpublished study.

the same. However, some classes of drugs prescribed in one facility were not used in the other. For example, phenothiazines were used more frequently in one service than in the other.

Drug prescribing is related to the social characteristics of patients as well as to those of doctors. Physicians are more likely to prescribe psychoactive drugs for women than for men, and women are more likely to medicate themselves than are men. A national survey conducted in May 1967 found that twice as many women (31 per cent) as men (15 per cent) had used psychoactive agents during the preceding twelve-month period.[11] Also, specific classes of drugs, minor tranquilizers such as Librium and Miltown, were more likely to be prescribed for women than for men. There were also major differences in psychoactive drug use among religious and racial groups. The same survey found that Jews use psychoactive drugs considerably more than do Catholics or Protestants and that the percentage of Negroes using psychoactive drugs is only about one half (13 per cent) that of whites (26 per cent).[12]

The objective of the survey was to construct a picture of psychoactive drug use in this country. The differences reported probably primarily reflect differential patterns of drug giving by physicians. But physicians can prescribe psychoactive agents only to those who seek and have access to their services. Since women are more likely to visit a physician or clinic than are men, they are also more likely to be given drugs. And Jews, on the whole, seem to

[11] H. J. Parry, "Use of Psychotropic Drugs by U.S. Adults," *Public Health Reports,* 1968, *83* (10).
[12] *Ibid.*

have traditionally placed great value on health and medical care, and medicine and its practioners have traditionally been held in esteem by them, so they too are likely to be placed on drugs. On the other hand certain minority groups do not have full and ready access to medical services and are not able to afford the services of private physicians. Furthermore, members of minority groups, as has been pointed out by Anselm Strauss and others, tend to be wary of medical services and medical personnel. It would, therefore, be remiss to seek the explanation for drug use in a traditional analysis of the motivations of individual members of different social groups without taking note of the link between an individual as a consumer of medical services in general and his likelihood of being given psychoactive agents.

IV

The Vicious Cycle
of Mystification

The relationship between the pharmaceutical industry and the medical profession is a very close one. Together they constitute an interlocking economic, scientific, professional, and educational network. Unfortunately, the symbiotic relationship between these two groups has consequences that do not always parallel the public interest and indeed may impede a rational understanding of the functions and uses of drugs. It is in the interest of both of these groups to maintain large numbers of persons on drugs, and it is especially important for the manufacturers to recruit new groups to drug use and to find new uses for their product. It is, moreover, in the interest of both groups to define more and more problems as medical in order to justify both the medical model and the intervention with drugs.

The industry relies upon the medical profession to sell its products through prescription and by virtue of medical authority, and it sees the physicians as its primary market. It also depends upon the medical profession for introducing new drugs and new drug uses and for policing its products to provide early warnings of possible dangerous or untoward effects.

The pharmaceutical industry maintains an extensive flow of information to the medical profession about its products and supplements direct advertising with generous free supplies of samples of both established and experimental drugs. In addition, the industry attracts the attention of physicians through its own journals, magazines, films, and newsletters, many of which are extremely impressive and intriguing. In this literature, information about drug products is interspersed with general medical news, stimulating articles of general intellectual and professional interest, and helpful hints about medical economics. The industry is also very active in and a source of financial support to medical education, and it sponsors many scientific conferences and meetings. Pharmaceutical houses often underwrite science writers who emphasize the accomplishments of medicine and of particular physicians to the general public. Scientific reports on specific drugs (psychoactive drugs among them) are often written by staff writers employed by the industry and are based upon information supplied to them by physicians remunerated by the pharmaceutical firm to assess the drug which it hopes to be able to market.

Like other professionals, physicians must depend in the main upon their journals for information regarding bona fide developments in the field of medicine and therapeutics. But these journals, apparently published by disinterested scientific associations and controlled by boards of medical experts, are themselves largely dependent upon the pharmaceutical industry for financial support. For example, James Faulkner, chairman of the Publications Committee of the Massachusetts Medical Society, which publishes the *New England Journal of Medicine,* reported that during 1968 revenue from advertising in the journal amounted to $2,241,544, while revenue from subscriptions amounted to only $662,328.[1] It can hardly be doubted that drug advertising accounted for most of this income. An examination of the October 1970 issue of *Archives of General Psychiatry,* published by the American Medical Association, revealed that ninety-eight pages were devoted to scientific articles (including the table of contents and related material) and that eighty-two pages were taken up by advertising, of which seventy-three and a half pages consisted of drug ads. These ads (twenty-three of which averaged 3.2 pages in length) were devoted almost entirely to praising the value of prescribing specific psychoactive agents.

No one knows exactly what calculations enter into a doctor's therapeutic decisions. . . . Ideally he relies on research findings and on the clinical experience of experts accumulated over the years and published in the medical literature, tempered by his own judgment and his knowledge of the patient's particular circumstances. All of us have the duty to be aware of new information and to reevaluate our therapeutics in its light. This is a humbling experi-

---

[1] R. C. Pillard, statement before the Subcommittee on Monopoly of the Select Committee on Small Business, July 30, 1969 (Washington, D.C.: Government Printing Office, 1969), p. 5413.

ence. We constantly see our highest hopes and strongest clinical impressions dissolve when hard evidence is collected. . . . An attitude of skepticism and respect for evidence is difficult to maintain. . . . My concern is that drug companies with all the resources they have to prompt doctors to prescribe drugs will just overwhelm the more conservative point of view. This is happening.[2]

Thus, the pharmaceutical industry, the mass media, physicians, and patients are wittingly or unwittingly locked in a vicious cycle of mutual mystification in which the problems of the human condition are increasingly medicalized. The chain of events constituting this cycle of mystification is held together by a set of highly complementary expectations.

It has been estimated that 60 per cent of the patients who appear in a general practitioner's office or clinic do so for largely nonmedical reasons.[3] They come because they are lonely, depressed, anxious, dissatisfied, or unhappy. They are troubled because they are finding it difficult or impossible to measure up to prevailing social prescriptions and ideologies as to what one ought to get out of life. They are not as popular, successful, sweet-smelling, thin, vigorous, or beautiful as they have been led to believe they ought and deserve to be. In effect, they are in a physician's office because of the premium contemporary society places upon appearance, mood, or perfor-

[2] *Ibid.*, p. 5408.
[3] R. Rabkin, *Inner and Outer Space* (New York: Norton, 1970).

mance; they are there because they feel they should be something other than what they are. It is only too true, as John Corry says, that "there is no end to the ways in which Americans can be manipulated and made to feel that there is something wrong, and that whatever it is, it can be solved by something or someone." [4]

Mystification is twofold here; the first level concerns the mythical ideals of health, normality, and functioning to which members of our society are exposed, and the second, the notion that failure to live up to these should be remedied through the medium of the medical establishment. Precisely those persons who are most uninvolved and chronically unsatisfied are most likely to become aware of small aches and pains and minor alterations in their body states; to these people the medical solution appears to be the most appealing. Physicians are all too often convinced that more and more of all forms of human unhappiness fall within their province, as depicted in a *New Yorker* cartoon which shows an impatient physician remarking to his patient: "O.K. O.K. You're entitled to a few pains. What else bothers you?" [5] Richard Rabkin describes this process insightfully in a chapter aptly entitled "The Healing Fictions": [6]

If there were someplace or someone to go to for help with ordinary unhappiness, the daily problems of living, there would probably be a sharp

[4] "The Politics of Style," *Harper's*, 1970, *241* (1446), 64.

[5] July 1970.

[6] *Op. cit.*, pp. 166–170.

42

reduction in nonmedically motivated visits to physicians and the distribution of pharmaceutical placebos. . . . For instance, when a health clinic was opened on the premises of a "little city hall" to which the public could take their social complaints, it was found that 60 per cent of the medical patients were sent there instead of being treated for physical ailments. This process can turn into an endless cycle, especially when patient and doctor fail to agree on a treatable medical complaint. Someone is vaguely distressed; because of lifelong contact with physicians, advertising, or other social influences, he shapes his complaint in terms of a medical model. *If this does not alleviate his distress, he eventually reaches a psychiatrist.* [Emphasis ours.]

Conscientious physicians who adhere to the medical canon "No treatment without a diagnosis" find it difficult to work with patients for whose complaints they can find neither a specific cause nor a satisfactory diagnosis. In such cases, being able to arrive at the diagnosis of psychogenic disorder neatly solves the dilemma. Other physicians, especially those who are young and eager to practice the skills they have been taught, initially experience great frustration in having to accept such individuals as patients. But although they may harbor reservations as to whether the patient has arrived at the proper place or whether they are, in fact, competent to render a medical service to him, they do not, for a variety of reasons, always have the option of turning him away. For these patients, the pharmaceutical industry provides a workable model within which the physician may practice comfortably by redefining the problems such patients bring as legitimate medical complaints. Indeed, the industry is ingenious in inventing illnesses and cures for such questionable complaints. One drug company, possibly with tongue in cheek, even invented and advertised a malady they called The Blahs and sold its own product as the specific cure. The appeal of the position of the pharmaceutical industry regarding the uses of psychoactive agents is that it offers physicians a rationale that legitimizes their medical intervention and treatment of problems which are nonmedical in origin. By treating the patient's emotional discomfort with drugs, the physician defines the patient's complaint as a medical one and, in so doing, legitimizes the doctor-patient relationship.

At the same time, the pharmaceutical industry continues to offer the public more and more over-the-counter drugs for every conceivable human condition and, in its advertising of them through the mass media, continues to provide the public with further reinforcement of the erroneous redefinition of human problems as medical ones. The pharmaceutical industry thus mystifies both physicians and the public. The physicians in turn mystify both themselves and their patients, though sometimes unwittingly and with good intention. And thus the vicious cycle of mystification is maintained.

Illegal Drug Use
and Mystification in
the Youth Culture

ﷺﷺﷺﷺﷺﷺﷺﷺﷺ

Their convictions and protestations to the contrary, young people often employ psychoactive drugs in ways and for purposes which are not dissimilar to those promulgated by the pharmaceutical industry and the medical profession and which are analogous to the way in which many adults use alcohol. Young persons use drugs to accomplish functions and to achieve states which, in the normal course of human development, arise from participation in human relationships and interactional processes. Drug taking for the young (as well as for adults) is undertaken to facilitate human interaction and to provide new or missing experiences. Drugs are taken in the pursuit of novelty and drama; to generate feelings of closeness, warmth, and awe of man and nature; and even to generate an experience of the uncanny, the horrible, the magical, and the loathsome.

Feeling alienated by an increasingly fragmented and ghettoized [1] society, the spokesmen for the youth counter-culture have adopted an ideology which legitimizes the use of drugs (much as do advertisements of the pharmaceutical industry) for the solution of the psychological and social problems besetting contemporary man. Here too we find the familiar denial of the propositions that drugs exact costs, that these sometimes outweigh benefits, that the use of drugs often leads to an erosion of the very qualities of relatedness and experience for which they are taken, that drugs engender undesirable psychological and social side effects (not to speak of the physiological ones), and finally that opting for a chemical solution obscures the nature of the real problems facing young people and can impede recognition that social systems need to be altered or that new social arrangements need to be created.

In this chapter we address our attention to the function drug taking serves; what it is about drugs which makes them appear to be the equivalents of experience and relatedness; and finally to what extent those who advocate and accept this solution engage in self-mystification.

To fully understand the attraction that the giving and taking of psychoactive drugs have to the young, one must appreciate the absolutely essential role that interaction plays in normal human development. Human beings are characterized by their strivings for and dependence upon interaction with other human beings. Such interaction is an end in itself, and interactional deprivation leads to anguish, loneliness, and depression. Interaction defines and

[1] A. Silberman, University of Cologne, personal communication.

affirms the humanness of the self. One acquires identity by being socially recognized and responded to
by another person. Interaction also defines and re-
defines the self and the social roles of interactors and
authenticates the identity assumed by an individual
vis-à-vis other persons.[2]

Many drugs, especially psychoactive drugs,
can produce rapid effects, can quickly alter behavior,
perception, and performances in the interaction
process. Two drinks can transform a socially inept
individual at a cocktail party or bar into one of the
boys, talking, touching, and moving with energy and
animation. But while he may believe that he is interacting successfully with other group members,
some of those whom he approaches so rapidly and
sometimes so unskillfully may perceive his behavior
rather differently. Such misperception under the influence of psychoactive agents often leads to self-
deception, especially with regard to the value of
one's performances.

Drugs achieve these effects or other ends by
bypassing meaning and means. They facilitate what
may be called the experience of effects. Thus, when
one effects ends through the use of drugs, one bypasses the usual experiences by which such ends are
normally accomplished. But although the ends may
be experienced as the same, the means through
which they have been achieved are different, and so
indeed is the outcome. When one attains intimacy
by means of drugs, one bypasses the usual phases of
relationship and interaction that occur on the road

[2] H. L. Lennard and A. Bernstein, *Patterns in
Human Interaction: An Introduction to Clinical Sociology*
(San Francisco: Jossey-Bass, 1969).

to true intimacy. One omits the process that is essentially a part of every genuine friendship. The pseudointimacy established with drugs is likely to vanish with the elimination of the drug or is at best so fragile that it cannot survive the stresses that beset any close relationship. So too with "mystical" experiences achieved by means of drugs. Here one bypasses all the usual preparatory focused activity and skills through which such mystical experiences have traditionally been achieved—for example, long periods of meditation, fasting, exercise, and even self-flagellation.

As suggested above, drugs tend to dissolve boundaries or distinctions among persons. They provide the user with a sense of closeness, community, and communion, of being in touch with people. Through the use of drugs such as marijuana and alcohol, the user feels he instantly achieves the intimacy and relatedness which ordinarily come about as a result of the normal "interactional dance" involving mutual self-revelation, learning about the other, becoming sensitive and attuned to each other, and establishing a common history of experience and points of contact. The drug user settles on the effect for effect's sake, bypassing involvement and social learning. But if human closeness is achieved only through drugs, one does not acquire the skills necessary to achieve these states in the absence of drugs, with the result that all that one has learned is how to create such states through the use of drugs.

Perhaps the youthful drug user has accepted the drug solution because other roads to human relatedness and social experience are closed to him, as a result of deficits in interactional skills and in his inner life. But if this is true for many educated middle-class youth, where should we look for an explanation? Modern society, especially American society, although technologically advanced, is interactionally barren, devoid of drama and ritual, of magic and mystery. The individual is overwhelmed with informational inputs, such as television, radio, motion pictures, newspapers, which distance him further and further from personal experience with other human beings. What one learns from television, for example, is how to look like someone who has a certain position, job, or role in society. One observes the visual appearance, the costume, the trimmings, and the behavior. The outward form can be and is imitated, but one cannot learn through such limited interaction how to think, feel, and relate to others in reciprocal roles; these can be learned only through participation in the process of interaction itself, through practice with a variety of different role partners (old, young, mother, father, persons similar and different from oneself). Interacting with each provides increments of knowledge about and experience with human relationships.

Learning is an inevitable accompaniment of human interaction. Briefly, what is learned in the course of a prolonged, complementary human relationship is that human beings enact roles; that is, there are groups of behaviors which are characteristic of persons in similar statuses (old, young, male, female). Such knowledge provides the primary context within which individuals learn how to get to know and to understand persons different from themselves. In the course of this human interaction inevitable problems arise—problems like how to achieve intimacy and empathy and problems of how to resolve differences with respect to dominance, submission, activity, and passivity. Practice in relating to others sharpens one's ability to detect deception or dishonesty and enhances one's behavioral repertoire. Different interactional behavior can be tried on for size, to see whether it facilitates and deepens relatedness. An "as if" and playful quality of interaction can be alternated with serious goal-directed proceedings.[3] These outcomes of experiencing the process of interaction lead to what is popularly characterized as depth versus shallowness.

Human depth does not come from exposure to visual experience alone, as, for example, in the spectator role into which television casts its viewers. After all, the television medium necessarily alters one's sense of time and of duration. On television whole human dramas are enacted within the limits of an hour or even less. Human experience is turned on and turned off at will, irrelevancies (advertisements) punctuate the evolving themes, and the spectator is encouraged to alternate between withdrawal and involvement at demand. A generation of young people reared by such a medium finds it difficult to participate in prolonged human relationships.

Watching television, then, merely provides samples from life; it is a far cry from the real thing. Hence, when an individual moves into an actual social context, he may be able to look the part and speak the lines of the script, but the experiential structure and emotional mode are not part of this act. The perfectly dressed, perfectly articulate per-

[3] *Ibid.*

former in the visual, even acoustical, mode may be-entirely illiterate at the interactional, experien-tial, and feeling levels. Not having practiced the in-teractional mode—in order to feel something, to overcome something, to be something; to come to terms with fear, shyness, love, or loneliness; to make any contact at all—he finds drugs provide a readily available solution for him. T. Roszak concludes his insightful discussion on youthful drug use with these words: [4]

> *"Better Things for Better Living Through Chemistry."* So reads one of the prominent hippy buttons, quoting E. I. Du Pont. But the slogan isn't being used satirically. The wearers mean it the way Du Pont means it. The gadget-happy American has always been a figure of fun because of his facile assumption that there exists a technological solution to every human prob-lem. It only took the great psychedelic crusade to perfect the absurdity by proclaiming that personal salvation and the social revolution can be packed in a capsule.

Human interaction embodies not only a com-plex of different levels and channels but different sensory modalities as well. Persons interact through such media as sight, sound, touch, and smell. Al-though each occasion for human contact may simul-taneously involve any number of these, one or the other may constitute the primary modality of inter-action at any one time. Optimal and satisfactory

[4] *The Making of a Counter Culture* (Garden City, N.Y.: Doubleday, 1969), p. 177.

51

human interaction requires the use of all sensory modalities, with appropriate balances among them. No one modality can either be relied upon exclusively or be neglected. Dependence on a single modality restricts the richness of interaction and limits the possibilities for human experience which can grow out of it.

The popularity of encounter groups and sensitivity training groups is testimony to the hunger for interaction as well as to the need for expression in underutilized sensory modalities. The title of Jane Howard's book on this growing movement is *Please Touch*,[5] though she might have just as aptly called it *Permission to Touch*. One major theme running through the variety of new social arrangements and experiments designed to promote growth and self-development is that of the necessity for human interaction to involve modalities other than the verbal and symbolic. Hence these new arrangements generally involve the construction of social contexts in which the balance of modalities is shifted. For example, special emphasis is usually shifted to the tactile modality of interaction, a mode of interaction generally underutilized in English-speaking cultures.

One general property of psychoactive drugs is that they shift the balance in the modalities or channels through which interaction occurs. Given classes of drugs in general have similar effects upon this shift. Users of hallucinogenic drugs, for example, stress increased awareness of sensory modalities (sound, vision, touch). Drugs tend to close off some channels and to open others. For example,

[5] (New York: McGraw-Hill, 1970).

drugs employed in the management of mental patients, such as the phenothiazines, tend to decrease the use of the kinesic (body movement) and para-kinesic (vocal qualities such as pitch, volume, rhythm) modalities.

Persons interacting under the influence of the same psychoactive agent tend to exhibit similarity in the modalities within which they find interaction facilitated and consequently in their expectations of each other. In other words, they become more interactionally attuned to each other. If we accept the proposition that interaction is mutually regulated, then we will find interaction among group members who are not tuned into the same channels awkward and mutually unsatisfying. Without such mutuality individuals have difficulty communicating with each other. Interaction between a person on a drug and one off can be compared to interaction in a tennis game in which one person is using a tennis racket and the other a ping-pong paddle. The trajectory, velocity, and timing are so different that a satisfying interactional experience becomes impossible.

This analogy explains why members of a family have difficulty interacting with a patient on phenothiazine or why nondrug users have difficulty interacting with those who have been turned on. It also explains the drop out or rather the drop in phenomenon of youthful drug users and the oft-noted desire of drug takers to turn on their nonuser friends and interactional partners, whether to the use of marijuana, LSD, or alcohol. Human beings in general prefer to interact with persons who have something in common with them. The colloquial expressions *turned on* and *turned off* acquire a new meaning in this context, for they appear to refer to the opening up or closing off of modalities of communication. This changing of modalities partly explains the pressure upon a drug-free person to ingest a drug when he wants to get in tune with people who are on drugs and the dissonance between the drug culture and the rest of society.

Despite the fact that the ingestion of psychoactive agents appears to open up sensory modalities and to facilitate interaction by dissolving boundaries, by aligning expectations, and by attuning modalities of communication, it appears to us that the interaction thus facilitated does not have quite the same properties as drug-free interaction. It is, in our view, more of a pseudointeraction than an authentic one.

Although a value judgment is clearly implied in this conclusion, it follows directly from our conception of the process involved in human interaction and relatedness. Our view is that this process entails responsiveness, mutuality, and feedback loops. Authentic human interaction requires sensitivity to other persons, recognition of boundaries, and, probably most significantly, phase differentiation. That is to say, the interactional process is progressive. It changes its character and the character of its participants over time.

The accomplishment of the purposes for which any group is formed requires different patterns of performances on the part of the group members during different phases of the process. For example, during the first phase of the formation of a theatrical group, the members are engaged in play selection, casting, and planning. During the next phase they are engaged in rehearsal and scenery construction, and, during the final phase, they are engaged in performances on stage. The purposes and goals for which individuals interact in groups require a phase differentiation of action through time. It does not appear to us that interaction while under the influence of drugs exhibits the full-fledged development of these qualities. This lack of change explains why, after repeated experiences with the so-called nonaddicting psychedelic drugs, users become dissatisfied. They become, to paraphrase Ken Kesey, "tired of opening the same door." [6] Nor does it appear to us that a group of people under the influence of drugs who are oblivious to the fact that one member is seriously ill and pleading for help have truly achieved communion with each other.

Psychoactive drugs, especially those legally prescribed, tend to restrain individuals from behavior and experience that are not complementary to the requirements of the dominant value system. The increase in their use in the youth culture paradoxically has coincided with the emergence of new cultural values from which few of us have escaped and which are so well summarized by the injunction to "keep your cool." These values are clearly congruent with the new technological environment in which deviance and difference are stressful.

The growing homogenization of modern life requires individuals who can conform with the most delicately and precisely timed technological schedules. Whether an individual is equipped to handle

[6] Quoted in T. Wolfe, *The Electric Kool-Aide Acid Test* (New York: Farrar, Straus, and Giroux, 1968), p. 355.

the day or not, he must have the appearance of being able to do so. He must not "blow his stack" or "fly off the handle" or show excess reactivity or involvement. The close relationship between drug taking and the avoidance of emotional involvement is only too profoundly anticipated in the slogans of Aldous Huxley's *Brave New World:* "A gramme in time saves nine," and "Remember that a gramme is better than a damn."

Mystification in the
Judgement of Drug Effects

ᔖᕽᔖᕽᔖᕽᔖᕽᔖᕽᔖᕽᔖᕽᔖᕽᔖᕽ

Although research by social scientists has suggested that specific experiences resulting from the use of illegal drugs, such as marijuana, are socially learned, social scientists do not appear to question the assumption that psychoactive drugs prescribed within the context of medical practice have the specific effects they are prescribed for. Social scientists appear to be reluctant to trespass upon what they evidently believe to be within the purview of the practice of medicine. But to comprehend the issues involved, it is essential to bear in mind a distinction between pharmacological effects and behavioral effects of psychoactive agents.

Basic scientists, especially pharmacologists, biochemists, and physiologists, have been accumulating evidence for the view that though drugs may have specific physiological effects, their effects upon behavior and experience are largely nonspecific. Still, their careful formulations have not had much success in revising deeply rooted, prevalent misconceptions of drug effects. The notions that psychoactive drugs exercise specific effects on behavior and experience and that these can be identified by the user are widely held by physicians and drug users, with regard both to prescribed and to illegal drugs. This erroneous model of the action of psychoactive drugs, accepted by professionals and nonprofessionals, is relentlessly reinforced by the media.

An important element in this erroneous model (that psychoactive drugs lead to specific experiential and behavioral effects) is the widespread belief, especially among youthful drug takers, that the drug user is an accurate source of knowledge about the effects of drugs. After all, should not the user himself be the one best informed about his own experiences and his own behavior? While we do not question that sometimes the judgments of a patient taking prescribed drugs or of persons using drugs outside a medical framework constitute a source of information about drug effects, we think ample evidence indicates that such judgments are often incomplete and sometimes wholly erroneous.

To be able to evaluate the effect of a psychoactive drug, a user must first establish a cause and effect relationship between the drug he has taken and the changes in behavior or experience which he is noticing. This relationship is readily misjudged. Individuals may attribute changes in feelings and behavior or relief of symptoms to the taking of a drug when the pill they have ingested is actually chemically inert (when they have taken sugar pills or other placebos). Physicians are fully aware of and indeed make use of the placebo phenomenon but fail to see the broader implications of the placebo effect and how it relates to the larger issue of misperception and misjudgment of so-called drug effects. A number of studies have found that over a third of the individuals given an inert substance report drug effects.[1] After having ingested a placebo, such individuals report relief from discomfort and pain, relinquish the symptoms for which the medication is given, or acquire new symptoms which they ascribe to the "drug."

Not infrequently patients report beneficial effects of drugs only minutes after a drug has been ingested, that is, within a time limit too brief for the drug to have dissolved in the stomach and to have diffused into circulation—within a time too short for a true pharmacological effect to have occurred. Such placebo phenomena can be ascribed to the fact that patients have learned to associate the administration of a drug with the promise of relief from illness, pain, or discomfort. The taking of a drug therefore mobilizes and actualizes an individual's expectations of change and relief from distressing symptoms.

Changes in experience, feeling, or perception also occur when the drugs the user believes he is taking are stimulants or hallucinogenic drugs. In one of the few major studies of the effects of marijuana Reese T. Jones undertook to investigate "one myth that has to do with the ability of the experienced user to judge the drug's quality."[2] He com-

---

[1] For a most comprehensive review of the research on the placebo phenomenon, see H. K. Beecher, *Measurement of Subjective Responses, Quantitative Effects of Drugs* (New York: Oxford University Press, 1959).

[2] "Marijuana Myths," unpublished manuscript, Langley Porter Neuropsychiatric Institute, San Francisco.

pared the subjects' abilities to judge the potency of the drug with that of an inactive placebo. Although the placebo lacked any of the ingredients that would make it psychoactive, only eleven of eighty subjects who smoked it judged it to be inactive. Ten chronic marijuana users who claimed to have used marijuana every day for over a year were asked to rate the material on a scale of 0 to 100, zero being "inactive material" and 100 being the "best marijuana I ever had." Their mean rating of the active material was 66, but their mean rating for the inactive material was 57—not significantly different.

A most interesting sidelight of this experiment concerns the nature of the placebo employed. Everyone was able to distinguish the smell and taste of marijuana from those of hemp stalk, oregano, catnip, and tansy. To produce the placebo effect it was necessary to use something that smelled and tasted like marijuana but from which the active ingredient (tetrahydrocannabinol—THC) had been removed. Jones concludes:

> *There may be an important learned component to the total experience associated with smoking cannabis so that when one is provided the taste and smell cues, the characteristic psychological state is induced, particularly in individuals primed for it. In support of this is the fact that the most experienced users are most "susceptible" to the effects of the placebo material. We've also observed that subjects with impaired taste and smell because of a cold or occluded nose can more readily distinguish the placebo than active material.*

When pharmacologically active agents are involved, users often report effects from the ingestion of the drug which are unlikely to have eventuated from that particular drug or class of drugs; for example, a user may report energizing effects from the administration of a drug with a pharmacologically sedating action.

When a person is uninformed about which drug has been administered to him or what the action of the drug is "supposed" to be, he generates his own expectations, and these in turn influence the degree of his response to the drug. C. M. Wilson and P. Huby,[3] in a study using English subjects in Liverpool, found that when "the subjects guessed correctly which class of drug (stimulant, depressant, or tranquilizing drug) they had received, they responded to it more vigorously; when they guessed incorrectly, the effects of the drug were partially or completely inhibited."

Among other myths widely shared by professionals and drug users is the idea that one can detect whether a drug has been taken and can identify which drug it is. We studied evaluations made by members of twenty-eight discussion groups in which one of the participants in each group had been administered 50 mg of chlorpromazine (a not inconsiderable dose), a major drug of the phenothiazine class (a class of drugs mainly used for its tranquilizing action on seriously disturbed individuals).[4] The

[3] "An Assessment of the Responses to Drugs Acting on the Central Nervous System," *Clinical Pharmacology and Therapeutics,* 1961, 2 (5), 587–598.

[4] H. L. Lennard, L. J. Epstein, and B. G. Katzung, "Psychoactive Drug Action and Group Interaction Process," *Journal of Nervous and Mental Diseases,* 1967, *145,* 69–78.

other members of each group received a placebo. Each group member was asked to determine for himself and the other group members whether the drug given had been a tranquilizer, a stimulant, or a placebo. Forty-five per cent of the group members who had received a placebo were judged to have received a tranquilizer by their cogroup members, and an additional 10 per cent of the members were thought to have been given a stimulant. Subjects who had received the chlorpromazine were judged to have received no drug at all in 21 per cent of the cases and a stimulant in 28 per cent of the cases. The study also included tape-recording and filming the subjects so that the psychiatric staff of the institute where the study was being conducted could observe the interaction. Psychiatrists were quick to inform us who among the subjects had, in their opinions, received the active agent. They were more often wrong than not.

While it is interesting to observe that it is not easy to detect the effects of drugs upon others, the more important issues are that individuals are likely to misjudge whether they themselves have received an active drug and that they report different effects depending on which drug they believe they have taken. Such consistent misjudgments of drug effects demand an explanation, and while it is true that human beings are suggestible, it is not sufficient or satisfying to explain the misjudgments of drug effects (and the conviction with which they are maintained) as simply the result of suggestibility.

The additional formulation that appeals to us is a refinement of the conceptions of experience and self developed by George Herbert Mead and succinctly summarized by H. S. Becker, who writes:

> *Objects (including the self) have meaning for the person only as he imputes that meaning to them in the course of his interaction with them. The meaning is not given in the object but is lodged there as the person acquires a conception of the kind of action that can be taken with, toward, by, and for it. Meanings arise in the course of social interaction deriving their character from the consensus participants develop about the object in question.[5]*

Let us examine how this conception applies to understanding the experience of drug effects. The meaning of a drug experience derives in large part from the converging set of conditions that constitute the experiential context of the drug taker. This context of drug effects has many dimensions. The most salient of these are the attention to bodily processes, the need to label internal stimuli, the mobilization of expectancies, the gross biochemical effects, the quantity of the drug taken, the status of the drug given, and the nature of the social context surrounding the person while he is on the drug. We discuss here each of these dimensions in turn.

The taking of any pill, whether active or inert, alerts an individual to his physiological functioning and psychological state. Any variations in internal processes and sensations are therefore likely to be noticed and once felt are likely to generate a

[5] "History, Culture and Subjective Experience: An Exploration of the Social Bases of Drug-Induced Experiences," *Journal of Health and Social Behavior,* 1967, *8* (3), 163–176.

need to be recognized and labeled in terms which have meaning to the person—that is, in the sense of Dewey and Bentley's "the naming is the knowing." Any "normal bodily state will give rise to pressures to decide what is felt, to decide how these feelings are to be labeled." Effects thus experienced are likely to be attributed by the individual to the drugs that he has ingested.[6]

Although individuals differ in how attentive or inattentive they are to their bodies and to physiological stimuli and at what threshholds they take note of them, we are all aware of the body and its processes to some degree and to the extent that our attention is not otherwise occupied. Since the human organism is in a continuous state of flux (the heart beats, lungs breathe, muscles relax and contract), nerve endings continuously transmit sensations from all parts of the body to the sensorium, thus providing a reservoir of ready-made sensations to choose from. But we are aware of different aspects of our internal processes at different times, depending upon the position we assume, the movements we make, or our mental set to monitor certain activities and not others.

When such changes in sensation and experience are ascribed to an ingested drug, this ascription reinforces the assumption that a drug effect is occurring and mobilizes expectations that the effect predicted or suggested by significant others (physician,

[6] S. Schachter, "Interaction of Cognitive and Physiological Determinants of Emotional States," paper given at Symposium on Psychological Approaches to Human Behavior, Harvard Medical School, Cambridge, Mass., April 1963.

friend, pusher) is likewise about to be realized. One's past experiences with the same or similar drugs also reinforce expectations regarding present effects. In such a state of watchful readiness, a wide range of sensations and experiences are likely to be interpreted and labeled as consistent with an anticipated drug effect.

Drugs, especially in large doses, produce physiological changes which vary with the drug ingested. A large quantity of LSD triggers bodily reactions that are different from those produced by a large dose of chlorpromazine. Nonetheless, the experiential effects of even high doses of a particular drug are open to a range of interpretations depending upon the social context in which the drug is taken. The gross changes in experience that the physiological effects of psychoactive drugs engender become interwoven with an array of other inputs, and this total effect in turn leads to what the individual labels as his drug experience.

One may regard specific drugs as carrying what may be called a germ of amenability. But, as we have seen, this germ is always nonspecific and general. In the language of those who take drugs, such general effects are characterized as uppers, downers, and psychedelics. We already know from the Wilson and Huby study (previously cited) that when subjects correctly guess which class of drugs they receive, their response is amplified; whereas when they guess incorrectly, the effects are partially or completely damped.

Misjudgments of drug effects such as those we have catalogued here are likely to occur when the person offering a drug is esteemed as an authority (physician) or is a knowledgeable older person or friend and when others who have ingested the same drug (friends in the youth culture) have already provided detailed descriptions and advertisements of the expected effects.

The final dimension influencing a person while he is on a drug is the nature of the social context. Aside from the atmosphere of expectation implicit in any setting, when other participants know someone is on a drug, a variety of elements in the context contribute to the eventual experience: how the context is peopled (that is, who is present); the demands for response and action felt by the drug taker; the tasks he is required to perform; the amount of information he must process; and the physical surroundings to which he must relate.

In the light of the subtlety and complexity of the factors that influence a drug experience, it is not surprising that misjudgments of drug effects occur so routinely. Still it is of considerable interest that the myth of the knowledgeability of the drug user has been maintained so tenaciously for so long.

Visible and Invisible
Consequences

With regard to the immediate and long-range effects of drugs we can only repeat the statement attributed to a patient who said to his psychiatrist, "He who understands the situation is not fully informed." As illustrated in the previous chapter, persons taking or being given potent psychoactive drugs are often not able to connect the many alterations in their physiological, psychological, and social functioning with their ingestion of psychoactive drugs. But neither are individual physicians, especially if the changes occur in areas of the patients' lives not visible to them (at work and in the family). Often, even if physicians see such connections, they may not feel it to be in the best interest of a patient to draw his attention to them. For example, when impairments in sexual functioning are associated with the use of certain potent antipsychotic and antianxiety agents, a patient may become conscious of these but not relate them to the drugs. A physician, even if these side effects are reported to him—as often they are not—may decide not to inform the patient about their origin in order to make certain that the patient continues to take the medication. Yet not knowing the cause may further increase the psychological disability of the patient. Many other illustrations of unrecognized drug effects or costs can be cited. One can ask, for instance, how many individuals taking an amphetamine-barbiturate mixture for the treatment of obesity recognize that their lowered threshhold for conflict and increased irritability are related to the ingestion of these drugs.

In addition, the fact that individual patients can react idiosyncratically to the administration of a psychoactive drug prevents an assessment of advantages and disadvantages beforehand and obliges physicians to postpone evaluation until after the drug is administered. However, since the patient does not always make the necessary connections and since the physician is not always able to elicit the information he needs to arrive at an accurate conclusion regarding the dysfunctional consequences of taking a drug, such costs can go undetected.

Psychoactive drugs represent a new technology. In Marshall McLuhan's terms drugs are a new medium and can be conceived of as an extension of the biochemistry of the body in the metaphorical sense that a computer represents an extension of the brain or nervous system. One feature of a medium is that it has multiple effects. As McLuhan puts it, "Any extension, whether of skin, hand, or foot, affects the whole psychic and social complex." [1] This

[1] *Understanding Media: The Extensions of Man* (New York: McGraw-Hill, 1964).

observation is particularly appropriate for psychoactive drugs, which affect not only the whole of the
individual but his group of immediate significant
respondents as well. When sizable segments of a
population ingest drugs, new modalities of human
transaction are constructed. Introduction of this new
medium into a human group, if only to one person,
affects the entire immediate social system. But these
new modalities alter the balance of interactions and
relationships in ways we still know little about.

Because personal and social consequences result from a new technology, in conceiving of drugs
as a new technology we must ask just what this extension of biochemistry means. What new scale,
what imperceptible environment, is created by the
massive use of drugs? In many areas of modern life
technological progress is increasingly becoming a
Trojan Horse. Initially we see only the benefits of
new technologies and inventions, but gradually we
become aware of the array of hidden and invisible
costs they introduce. We need only consider the initially staggering and unquestionable benefits of
DDT in the eradication of malaria and the pro-
longation of life. The continued indiscriminate use
of DDT however is now threatening us with unforeseen ecological disasters. Early warnings regarding
such indirect consequences either were taken lightly
or were disregarded. Similarly disregarded were the
German physicians who alerted their colleagues to
the potentional dangers of thalidomide. Only after
more than 5000 children had been crippled were the
medical professionals in Germany and England able
to clearly recognize the effect of thalidomide on

fetal development.[2] The potential costs of the taking and giving of psychoactive drugs may not be on the same scale or as visible as those in the thalidomide tragedy, but one should very seriously consider in what sense the widespread and ever increasing use of psychoactive agents has unforeseen, unanticipated, and unintended consequences.

McLuhan claims that media tend to atrophy or amputate the functions they extend. He says that "any invention of technology also represents a 'self-amputation' of our physical bodies, and such extension also demands new ratios or new equilibria among the other organs and extensions of the body." [3] In what sense do psychoactive drugs amputate or atrophy the functions they extend? An important possibility is that the long-term use of psychoactive drugs of all kinds results in having the self-regulating function of the body amputated. Though *amputation* is perhaps too strong a term, in many persons a definite modification in this self-regulatory mechanism occurs.

To illustrate, if one becomes tired and subsequently rests, energy is restored and one is able to return to work. One grows tired again and rests again. If, on the other hand, one tires and takes amphetamine, the cycle takes a different course. The amphetamine restores a sense of being energetic, and rest is postponed. At night one feels wound up, drained, and irritable. In order to sleep, a sedative becomes necessary. The next morning the individual

[2] For an excellent discussion of the thalidomide tragedy see L. Gross, "The Tragedy of Thalidomide Babies: Preview of a German Horror Trial," *Look,* May 28, 1968.
[3] *Op. cit.*

is excessively fatigued and can meet his performance obligations only by taking another dose of amphetamines. In this way responsibility for the regulation of activity and rest has been taken over by the drugs. This pattern of drug use results in at least a temporary impairment of the ability of an organism to regulate its own energy expenditures and to deal with fatigue, perhaps resulting in a permanent disturbance of the self-regulatory function.

So far we have explored the amputation question only in terms of the individual's biochemical and psychological functioning. To the question "What functions are amputated by the taking of drugs?" we have proposed that it is the self-regulatory function of the body. But another interesting and potentially more important amputation occurs at the level of social interaction and concerns the group and its responsiveness to its own members. Drugs may well amputate or atrophy a group's ability to make provisions for and to develop strategies of human relatedness in response to particular psychological reactions among its members, such as anxiety, grief, rage, or to extreme forms of behavior.

Physicians commonly place individuals who have suffered a loss, such as the death of a relative, on heavy sedation. While the sedation enables the individual to enact his social obligations during the funeral and other ritual occasions, it deprives him of the full experience of grief, which, it is increasingly recognized, fulfills significant psychological functions. The sedation of a grieving individual places less strain on those having to relate to him, but we wonder too whether it does not deprive them of an opportunity to experience valued emotions such as closeness and empathy. In response to the question of whether it is more healthy for people to be reacting to or to be chemically protected from those emotions which are an inevitable part of a full and normal life, Daniel X. Freedman, chairman of the Department of Psychiatry at the University of Chicago, remarks that "grief is very important to normal experience, and . . . stunted grief, stunted emotional working through of these problems, can lead to a serious psychiatric problem." [4]

When a family sends one of its members to a physician for a sedative or when a ward psychiatrist prescribes chlorpromazine for an agitated inpatient, both, in effect, amputate the capacity of or at least render it unnecessary for respondents in the immediate social environment (the medical and nursing staff) to alter themselves and the pattern of their relationships to deal with extreme or deviant behavior. Drugs alter this basic human function for any group into which they are introduced—families, classrooms, work groups, hospital wards—and in the whole array of mental health institutions, drugs often amputate truly therapeutic functions.

The regulatory function is thus increasingly delegated to drugs, not to the significant parties in the interpersonal environment. We anticipate that the eventual cost in human group relatedness of the decision to substitute a drug modality for an interpersonal one will be high. The more potent the drug, the more sustained its use, the more likely is an increase in unanticipated and unwanted side effects.

[4] Testimony before the Subcommittee on Monopoly of the Select Committee on Small Business, July 1969 (Washington, D.C.: Government Printing Office, 1969).

Even during the early period of enthusiasm over the application of drugs to the management of psychological disturbances, many clinicians expressed concern about the possibility that psychoactive drugs might have long-range effects on the central nervous system. But these expressions of caution were largely unheeded, and the primary approach to managing severely disturbed patients was shifted to psychoactive drug "treatment." For a time it was believed that such side effects as were noticed would subside after the discontinuance of drugs or through administration of other drugs. This view must now be revised. The majority of mental patients in this country are being maintained on drugs, and with the passage of time the long-term effects of psychoactive drug administration are becoming increasingly visible.

A workshop sponsored by the Psychopharmacology Research Branch of the National Institute of Mental Health was called together in 1968 to discuss a new syndrome, referred to as tardive dyskinesia, which has come to be recognized in increasingly large numbers of hospitalized mental patients who have been maintained on certain classes of psychotropic drugs over long periods. Tardive dyskinesia is a central nervous system disorder, possibly with irreversible effects. Its manifestations include involuntary movements especially affecting the lips and tongue, hands and fingers, and body posture. Consequently, speech may be seriously affected, the face may become distorted and subject to uncontrolled expressions, and sustained normal posture may become impossible. Irreversible damage to enzyme systems, especially in older patients, may also result from prolonged drug usage. Aside from the physical limitations this damage imposes upon patients, the carry-over to his potential as an interactor is also serious. Thus the dysfunction is twofold, neurological and interpersonal. The chairman concluded the workshop meeting with these remarks:

> *During the last fifteen years drugs have been given to a large portion of psychiatric patients with little thought of what the risks are. The films of this workshop have shown a number of fairly severe cases of dyskinesia. But many such cases can be seen if one takes the trouble of walking through the wards of mental hospitals. I feel that we should revise our therapeutic approach with drugs as the risk seems to be considerable. Twenty to 25 per cent of the patients are afflicted by this disorder according to our observations; the disorder may last for many years or perhaps indefinitely in the more severe cases. Even if symptoms persist only for months or a few years in the milder cases, the problem still is of considerable clinical importance.*[5]

Iatrogenic maladies will probably always be with us. Tardive dyskinesia is only one of a long list of examples of new technological innovations

[5] G. E. Crane and R. Gardner, Jr. (Eds.), *Psychotropic Drugs and Dysfunctions of the Basal Ganglia: A Multidisciplinary Workshop,* Workshop Series of Pharmacology Section, NIMH, No. 3, Public Health Service Publication No. 1938 (Washington, D.C.: Government Printing Office, 1969).

which are disseminated with the greatest enthusiasm and which ultimately result in dysfunctional outcomes neither anticipated nor sought for. Neither the producers of new technologies nor physicians are omniscient. We are even sympathetic to the argument that despite the risks, for some patients under some circumstances today life-long administration of phenothiazine drugs may conceivably be the only option or the lesser evil. What is so disturbing to us, however, is the failure to learn from past errors. The drug industry, the medical profession, and the public at large do not seem to benefit from the lessons so apparent in this and other tragic illustrations.

As we see it, the lesson to be learned is that the effects of drugs are multiple and complex, and only a differentiated and sophisticated approach will lead the way to their proper use. Drug effects are both short range and long range, both visible and invisible, both specific and enormously diffuse. Those advocating the use of drugs must become sensitive to and aware of their multiple and aggregate effects, even if such investigation delays the introduction and use of new agents. Especially it is becoming clear that new priorities must be assigned to the social and psychological implications of drug use, perspectives that have hitherto been given little consideration by action-oriented practitioners. In 1964 one of us wrote: [6]

[6] H. L. Lennard, *A Proposed Program of Research in Sociopharmacology,* in P. H. Leiderman and D. Shapiro (Eds.), *Psychobiological Approaches to Social Behavior* (Stanford, Calif.: Stanford University Press, 1964), pp. 127–137.

Classical pharmacological techniques did not provide the means for studying the effects of drugs on individual and social behavior. The development of psychopharmacology permitted the study of drug effects on psychological functions and individual behavior. Attention must now be directed to the evaluation of drug action on interpersonal behavior systems and processes. Like the unanticipated effects of thalidomide on fetal development, there may be drug effects on specific behavioral systems that are currently being ignored. For example, there may be untoward effects of tranquilizing drugs on "parenting" and family function. There is the likelihood that new psychiatric syndromes will become apparent in children raised by parents who have been under chronic drug administration.

The time has come to assign a high priority to research that embraces the whole array of drug effects upon the individual, his family, and all the social networks within which drugged individuals interact. Scientists, educators, and physicians who insist that the major problem of drug misuse and untoward drug effects is merely that of the misuse of stimulants and hallucinogenic drugs by young people or one of the control of relatively minor side effects and who persist in dismissing as trivial or idealistic the model of drug misuse proposed in this book are evidently incapable of profiting from the tragic lessons to be learned from the history of drug use.[7]

[7] An interesting illustration of the costs of a wrong model

is provided by the fascinating book by Sir William J. Sinclair, *Semmelweis, His Life and His Doctrine* (Manchester at the University Press, 1909), subtitled, "A Chapter in the History of Medicine," and a tragic chapter it was indeed. In 1847 Ignaz Philipp Semmelweis discovered the cause of puerpal (childbed) fever, which took the lives of many women who were unfortunate enough to give birth in hospitals. He discovered that medical students and physicians carried the infection to their patients from the anatomy laboratory and the autopsy table. Semmelweis was able to demonstrate that by requiring students and physicians on his service to wash their hands, he could reduce the mortality from childbed fever drastically. The leading physicians of his day rejected Semmelweis and his evidence. For twenty years he was unable to convince most of his contemporaries in the field of medicine to take the simple step which would have saved countless lives. The attacks on him, the "scientific" refutations of what is now obvious, make fascinating reading. Sinclair's book is a classic exposition of the costs of a false model and an impressive documentation of the resistance to a new and unfamiliar idea. We can all profit from reading this chapter of medical history.

VIII

Toward New Models
of Drug Action

The descriptions of the effects of psychoactive drugs provided in advertisements and circulars to physicians and to the general public serve to perpetuate and deepen the mystification that surrounds the use of drugs to alter states of consciousness and regulate behavior.* Hence Librium is claimed to "reduce anxiety," Compoz to "calm the nerves," and Elavil to "lift depression." From this frame of reference, specific psychotropic drugs are described as directly altering specific emotional states and affecting specific psychological processes. This paradigm of drug action seems patterned largely after a traditional conception of drug specificity exemplified by Paul Ehrlich's 1906 notion of the "magic bullet," wherein a given chemical agent is believed to seek out a specific target in the organism.

If we picture an organism as infected by a certain species of bacterium, it will obviously be

* This chapter was coauthored by Steven D. Allen.

78

easy to effect a cure if substances have been discovered which have an exclusive affinity for these bacteria and act deleteriously or lethally on these and on these alone, while, at the same time, they possess no affinity whatever for the normal constituents of the body and cannot therefore have the least harmful or other effect on that body. Such substances would then be able to exert their final action exclusively on the parasite harbored within the organism and would represent, so to speak, magic bullets *which seek their target of their own accord.*[1]

Much contemporary research and theorizing about psychoactive agents (and certainly their application) still appear implicitly to be based upon this model of drug action, despite the fact that sophisticated psychopharmacologists would deny its validity. Although this approach has proved extremely useful in the management of many somatic states and particularly in the control of a wide range of infectious diseases with antibiotics, even within the framework of this conception of specific drug action it is well established that, with any agent, there is a diffusion of effects, generally referred to as side effects. René Dubos draws attention to some of the disturbances in organismic-ecological relationships resulting from drug use. He concludes that "even a highly selective drug is likely to react with some structure other than the one for which it has

[1] Address delivered at the dedication of the Georg-Speyer-Haus, September 1906, in F. Himmelwert (Ed.), *The Collected Papers of Paul Ehrlich,* Vol. 3 (London: Pergamon, 1960) , p. 59.

been designed. In other words, absolute lack of toxicity is an impossibility." [2]

An appropriate model of drug action is that, when a drug is introduced into a person, it produces alterations in the physiological system of the organism, some of them desirable and others undesirable. The desired effects are conventionally labeled the main effects, and all other changes are labeled side effects, regardless of whether they are positive, negative, uncomfortable, dangerous, or massive.

Drugs are sometimes relabeled when their side effects prove to be more interesting than their main effect. The history of psychoactive drugs is replete with such examples. Phenothiazine was initially used as a urinary antiseptic; and chlorpromazine was used to induce artificial hibernation to facilitate anesthesia during surgery, an action H. Laborit and P. Huegenard [3] term "pharmacological lobotomy." Only later were its psychoactive properties identified as its main attribute. The discoveries of the "specific" effects of lithium, the amphetamines, iproniazid, and others are similar.[4] The recognition that specificity of drug action is, to quite a considerable extent, a fiction created by such labeling processes would advance our understanding as

[2] "On the Present Limitation of Drug Research," in P. Talalay (Ed.), *Drugs in our Society* (Baltimore: Johns Hopkins Press, 1964), p. 41.

[3] H. Laborit and P. Huegenard, *Journal de Chirurgie*, 1951, *67*, 631.

[4] A. Hordern, "Psychopharmacology: Some Historical Considerations," in C. R. B. Joyce (Ed.), *Psychopharmacology* (Philadelphia: Lippincott, 1968).

well as contribute to the process of demystification.

In general, then, drugs not only affect the organs, functions, and processes to which they are directed, but they alter processes not intended to be so altered. Thus, antibacterial agents frequently change the balance of intestinal environments. Drugs designed to minimize tissue rejection tend to leave the organism less able to deal with viral and bacterial infectious processes. The nonspecificity of drug action is even more crucial in the case of psychoactive drugs. Drugs designed to change experience or behavior not only alter internal body processes, as revealed by the range of possible side effects, but also the complex of psychological and social processes connecting the individual to his physical and human environment.

One may anticipate that the diffusion effect of psychoactive drugs would be extraordinarily broad in the light of their goal of changing human experience or behavior. Unfortunately, equally extraordinary is the extent to which this problem has been oversimplified. It is usually dismissed as one of undesirable but minor side effects. This oversimplification may well be at the root of the neglect of this important issue. Furthermore, while other drugs are available to alleviate the unintended physical side effects of psychoactive drugs, the use of a similar strategy to control untoward, nonspecific psychological and social effects will most likely only extend the area of behavioral fallout. Giving a second drug to counteract an undesirable side effect of a primary drug results in a further diffusion of influence, which all too frequently only extends the problem we are calling attention to. The range of unanticipated experiential and behavioral consequences is increased. We are inclined to believe that further experience and investigation regarding the giving of methadone to counteract the effects of heroin will prove the wisdom of these observations.

The issue that must now bear the most exhaustive scrutiny is the application of the medical model of drug action as a rationale for the use of chemical agents to accomplish psychological (as opposed to physiological) alterations. In other words, what is the conceptual justification for the belief that specific chemical agents can be found and utilized to control and alter specific cognitive and emotional states? As Stanley Schachter [5] points out, the model of specific drug action does not discriminate between the physiological and the cognitive determinants of emotional states. Research, on the whole, does not support a purely visceral physiological formulation about emotion. On the contrary, as Schachter demonstrates, there is considerable evidence of the role played by cognitive and contextual determinants of emotional states. Schachter suggests:

A general (rather than specific) pattern of sympathetic discharge is characteristic of emotional states. Given such a state of arousal . . . one labels, interprets, and identifies this state in terms of the characteristics of the precipitating situation and one's apperceptive mass. . . . Cognitions arising from the immediate situa-

[5] "The Interaction of Cognitive and Physiological Determinants of Emotional States," in P. H. Leiderman and D. Shapiro (Eds.), *Psychobiological Approaches to Social Behavior* (Stanford, Calif.: Stanford University Press, 1964), pp. 138–173.

*tion as interpreted by past experience provide
the framework within which one understands
and labels one's feelings. It is the cognition that
determines whether the state of physiological
arousal will be labeled "anger," "joy," or whatever. . . . Given a state of physiological arousal for which an individual has no immediate
explanation, he will label this state and describe
his feelings in terms of the cognitions available
to him."*

The logic of this view is that however specific
the physiological and autonomic effects of a drug
may be, the cognitive-psychological effects are exceedingly variable. Within this frame of reference,
drugs alone do not trigger such specific affective reactions as fear, anger, depression, and joy. Specificity
of psychological effect, following Schachter, hardly
ever comes from the drug itself but comes from the
contextual cues surrounding the person whom the
drug has primed. Epinephrine injected in a neutral
context, for example, does not induce anger in experimental subjects.

The model appropriate to psychoactive drug
effects is more like the following. One takes a drug,
thereby introducing specific changes in his physiological state. These changes, however, do not trigger
specific or uniform psychological or behavioral consequences. A specific emotional response is then generated both by the social context (the surrounding
social and environmental cues) and by one's set
(one's past experiences with similarity patterned experience). How one labels this inner experience depends largely upon the nature of the situation and

knowledge of how similar feelings were labeled in the past. Thus, one is cognitively active in the structuring of physiological sensation and in the labeling of inner experience rather than serving as a passing recipient of an effect triggered solely by a biochemical substance.[6]

Psychoactive drugs frequently induce physiological effects which facilitate a range of interpretations of bodily states and specific mood changes. The popularity of many over-the-counter sedatives and tranquilizers may in large measure be due to the ease with which drowsiness, lassitude, and general physiological slowing can be interpreted and labeled as psychic tranquility. Interesting enough a major property of Valium (diazepam), one of the most commonly used minor tranquilizers, is its action as a muscle relaxant.[7] (It may also be noted that a major physiological effect of Spanish fly—cantharides—thought in folk lore to be an aphrodisiac, is irritation of the urinary tract. When this drug is given or taken to increase sexual excitement, the recipient is encouraged to interpret the increased irritability of the urethra and other sensations as a sign of the beneficial effect of the drug on the target function).

Just as the introduction of a drug produces a range of systemic alterations in the physiological system of an organism (alterations which require the individual to interpret and label them), so the administration of a psychoactive agent affects the social

[6] We are aware that the validity of this proposition is dose related.

[7] *Medical Newsletter,* 1969, *11* (20), 81–84.

systems in which the user participates and results both in changes in the system as a whole and in the interpretation of these changes by the participants. Any changes in the psychological state and social behavior of a member of a social system or group inevitably has consequences for the other members of that system and for the system as a whole. This diffusion of effects is hardly ever assessed by physicians when they administer a psychoactive agent.

When a psychoactive agent is introduced into a social system its effect diffuses throughout the whole system, and social behavior in the system into which a psychoactive agent is introduced is affected in a variety of ways. The employment of a psychoactive agent in a social system also changes expectations and attitudes. Both the user and the nonuser members of the system are changed. The introduction of psychoactive agents into mental hospitals, for instance, resulted in many indirect changes in the character of these hospitals and their staffs. Staff morale improved immeasurably. Perceiving patients as manageable produced "favorable" attitudes in the staff. Good prognoses attaching to mental patients have been attributed to the modification in the behavior of hospital staffs toward patients subsequent to the introduction of psychoactive medication. One may wonder whether the staff cooperation required for the development of the new therapeutic milieus or open hospitals would have been so readily forthcoming in the absence of their new expectations about "drugged" patients. Indeed it has been remarked that there might well be a "revolt" by mental hospital personnel were the use of psychoactive drugs curtailed.[8] Similar changes in expectations and attitudes have been described in the families of persons who have been placed on psychoactive medication.

While it appears almost self-evident to a social scientist that the administration of a psychoactive drug to a member of a social group will—if it changes that person's social behavior—inevitably have some effect on the behavior of others in the group with whom he is interacting, this assumption has not received much research attention. Some intriguing pilot studies by V. and H. H. Nowlis and by J. A. Starkweather [9] suggest that knowing which drug has been administered to the first member of a pair leads to a better prediction of changes in performance in the second member of the pair than in the first.

In our research we studied the effect of a single administration of a phenothiazine drug on patterns of interaction in seven "natural" groups, each of which contained three persons.[10] Only one member of each group was given phenothiazine. We noted a decrease of activity on the part of the

[8] Informal remarks, dinner meeting, American College of Neuropsychopharmacology, San Juan, Puerto Rico, December 1967.

[9] V. Nowlis and H. H. Nowlis, "The Description and Analysis of Mood," *Annals of the New York Academy of Science,* 1956, *65,* 345–355. J. A. Starkweather, "Individual and Situational Influences on Drug Effects," in R. M. Featherstone and A. Simon (Eds.), *A Pharmacologic Approach to the Study of the Mind* (Springfield, Ill.: Thomas), 1959).

[10] H. L. Lennard, L. J. Epstein, and B. G. Katzung, "Psychoactive Drug Action and Group Interaction Process," *Journal of Nervous and Mental Disease,* 1967, *145,* 69–78.

"drugged" member and a decrease in the number of communications addressed to him by the others. The other group members, each of whom was on placebo, uniformly increased the frequency of their interactions with each other.

Changes in the formal parameters of interaction reflect changes in significant aspects of social processes (adequacy of role performance, amount of decision-making power, strength of coalitions). Changes in a group setting may have serious consequences for group functioning. For example, a decrease in participation in decision-making on a job may have major consequences for an individual. A decrease of communications directed to a child by a mother who has been given phenothiazine medication may have implications for the operation of the family system as a whole. Such minor interactional deficits and redistributions of behavior may have major impacts on the functioning of social groups.

Administration of a psychoactive drug to a member of a social system (for example, a family) may directly or indirectly change the structure of the role relationships within the group as well as the group's relationships to larger social systems of which it is, in turn, a member. For example, psychoactive drugs may enable a family with a psychologically impaired member to retain that member. Through these means his role position is not vacated. But at the same time the retention in the family of an impaired (or "strange") member may change the family's relationship to other families and to the community.

When drug administration results in a family's retaining a member whose behavior reflects not only his "illness" but the effects of the drug treatment as well, it is difficult to differentiate between changes resulting from the patient's illness and those resulting from the psychoactive drugs. The hypothesis is advanced that drugs result in a rearrangement of family functions, the assumption being that the "ill" member on drugs tends to be excluded from normal family processes (such as decision-making and the resolution of daily problems). These rearrangements can reflect the presence of an "impaired" member in the family or can be the result of drug-induced damping of behavioral contributions or both.

Unfortunately, the mystification pervading the model of drug action permeates the implied model of treatment as well. Contemporary models of treatment rest on the logic that the problem of drug misuse, abuse, or addiction is a metabolic aberration or, at best, a problem of the person: his physiological or psychological characteristics, his motivational structures, and so on. Drug abusers and addicts are often described as having dependent and inadequate personalities with psychopathic character structures, or as seeking reassurance of their personal competence, confirmation of their identities, or status gains. Complementing these descriptions are treatment regimens focusing on the person's biochemical processes or his sense of self. The individual is conceived of as the unit of treatment, and effects are aimed at altering his internal make-up—from his metabolic balances to his personal dispositions and goals. Preoccupation with persons is certainly an improvement over preoccupation with chemicals; but even the person is not a sufficiently comprehensive frame of reference from which to construct a successful program of therapeutic intervention.

The goal of therapy is only too often devoted exclusively to reduction of the intake of a proscribed drug—even if this means addicting the patient to a comparatively higher dose of a chemically related (but not a psychically gratifying) drug that has social sanction. I. Chein describes this situation as follows: "Attention is so fixated on the drug that scarcely an eyebrow is lifted at the manifest paradox of patients' cooperating with a treatment regimen—whether it be methadone or a maintenance schedule of heroin —that deprives them of the psychic gratifications for the sake of which they are supposedly impervious to treatment and cure." [11]

The beliefs that the addiction problem resides in the addict and that the problem of drug abuse is created by the abuser have led to a situation in which persons who seek help are entreated, persuaded, cajoled, and "treated" to stop their drug taking. They are given varieties of psychotherapy, psychoanalysis, group therapy, aversion therapy, shock treatment, and are even institutionalized. Focusing exclusively upon individual personality and psychological make-up has led to every conceivable effort to deal with "him" and "his" drug problem. However ingenious, all these efforts which were focused on their bodies and their minds have

[11] "Psychological Functions of Drug Use," in H. Steinberg (Ed.), *Scientific Basis of Drug Dependence, A Symposium* (London: J & A Churchill, 1969), pp. 13–30.

yielded a record of success that is strikingly bleak.

But an alternative view, which we are suggesting, is that the problem of drug misuse does not reside within individuals and that, therefore, it cannot be solved by attention to individuals alone. If it is located anywhere, it exists somewhere in the complex relationship patterns of persons and their social contexts. Focusing upon the individual and searching for metabolic and intrapsychic explanations of his difficulties with drugs draws attention away from the larger pattern and leads to ineffective treatment efforts.

In the past, the transpersonal dimensions of the drug problem were passed over as influences which were regarded as important but which were not seen as the central question. A major conceptual figure-ground reversal of the problem is required. We suggest transindividual dimensions are more than influences and are in fact the very substance of the drug abuse problem. They sustain it more effectively than does any individual's physiological tolerance or personal motives. A tough social homeostasis has developed one in which patterns once established tenaciously resist change. Existing social patterns have recruited large number of persons into excessive drug use, and social sequences for keeping them there have become institutionalized. Treatment agencies have, unfortunately, become an integral part of this pervasive social system.

For almost all members of American society, some form of drug taking (from aspirin to heroin) has become a regular component of personal self-regulation and daily life; and the use of drugs (from alcohol to marijuana) has become an essential constituent of social interaction in which persons routinely participate. Mass and local media keep drugs constantly in view and make them our daily companions, capable of producing virtual miracles. In American society drugs have become as common as clothing, and a similar kind of dependency has come into existence. For many persons, to be stripped of their pharmacological wardrobe would be tantamount to facing the world naked. Yet to describe persons as being dependent upon or addicted to clothing because they suffer without it does not accurately characterize the situation. The sustaining forces in both instances—in both the use of drugs and the use of clothing—do not reside inside the individual person; they reside in the whole context of events that sustain his current pattern of behavior.

The few programs of treatment and rehabilitation that have reported any degree of success seem to be based on a comprehensive model of addiction as located within a larger system of events and relationships. As an illustration we briefly review a program for the treatment and rehabilitation of chronic alcoholics developed by Robert O'Briant in San Joaquin County, California. This program extends the network and system implicit in the philosophy of Alcoholics Anonymous.

To appreciate the essential departure in this approach, let us briefly review the difficulties faced by an alcoholic who wishes to remain sober. His social-symbolic environment barrages him with messages containing the instruction to drink. The mass media carry many advertisements for alcoholic beverages. (The October 19, 1970, issue of *Newsweek,* for instance, contained 18 alcohol ads covering 17½ pages.) The alcohol industry expends approximately $200 million annually for advertising. Every day, he is confronted by billboard advertisements and brightly colored neon signs displayed by bars and cocktail lounges. In many states even supermarkets and drugstores display alcohol conspicuously, often in locations (the checkout counter) which are almost unavoidable.

In addition to commercial influences, social pressures operate in many interpersonal situations. The use of alcohol is normatively prescribed in everyday situations. Drinking alcohol is culturally associated with images of masculinity, sociability, and hospitality. It is rare that one visits friends, attends a party, or eats at a restaurant without being offered alcohol; and to refuse is often to create an awkward social situation. In many occupations and social networks, pressures to drink are especially intense. Businessmen drink when entertaining clients; restaurant and bar owners often share drinks with regular customers; cocktails are served to journalists at press gatherings; and for military personnel socializing and alcohol consumption are almost synonymous.

Neither the alcoholic nor those who attempt to help him are sufficiently aware of this powerful relationship between drinking and contextual events. Their perception of the problem is often limited by the "dermal illusion," [12] the idea that individuals are autonomous, self-activating units whose behavior is dictated by internal programs and is

[12] G. Bateson, comments at the Conference on Social Change (Princeton, N.J., December 1969).

relatively independent of context. This view leads them to perceive drinking as the result of hypothetical internal factors such as impulses or compulsions, rather than as a response to patterns of contextual events.

Once the interrelatedness of environmental message and response is accepted, it becomes evident that an alcoholic's drinking pattern cannot be readily changed without making changes in his physical and social contexts. He must be extricated from contexts in which the message to drink is present and placed in a context in which another set of messages is dominant. This is the strategy utilized by programs such as those developed by O'Briant. We shall not review the medical aspects of the program nor its emphasis on educating the alcoholic about the nature of alcohol and its physical effects. Of interest to us is how the program assumes responsibility for building a new social network for the alcoholic.

The reconstruction of the alcoholic's social landscape is accomplished in a residential treatment setting separate from the hospital at which the alcoholic first seeks help. Social interaction, both structured and unstructured, is encouraged by the structure of the program, such as limited size (fewer than fifty alcoholics at a time), daily group meetings, and the absence of offices for the staff into which they might retire and escape interaction with the alcoholics in residence.

The program subsequently makes available other social settings which facilitate the continuing association of sober alcoholics with each other so that they remain embedded in positive social networks. A steady schedule of group meetings and social activities is provided them as well as an opportunity to visit with former and present participants in the program and with the staff. Meetings are seen as being basic to the building of new social networks. They provide support and confirmation of the identity of each person in the program as an alcoholic and as a human being. The friendships and associations formed during participation in the program are seen as replacing those formerly held with one's drinking buddies.

The unit of intervention then has been moved from the individual to his relationships with others and to the construction of social contexts where the message "don't drink" prevails and is reinforced. These new social contexts facilitate changes in the individual's drinking behavior. Moreover, the drug option has been replaced by the option of authentic human interaction. The minimal social changes essential to maintenance of sobriety therefore include frequent association with sober alcoholics; nonsolitary living arrangements, preferably with other sober alcoholics; occupation of some sort, either employment or leisure activities —helping in the rehabilitation of other alcoholics is especially desirable; participation in an array of social activities while sober (many alcoholics have never attended a social function, made love, or related to coworkers and friends while sober).

These changes cannot be accomplished merely by telling the alcoholic to change. The treatment program itself must embody such changes by reterritorializing the social living space of the alcoholic through the provision of new social and physical arrangements.

Another example of a treatment program with a sophisticated and comprehensive view of the problem of drug addiction is the Phoenix House Program in New York City, under Dr. Mitchell Rosenthal. Here again the effort is directed at establishing new social networks and developing new interactional repertoires and skills, indeed at undertaking no less than to change the whole life style of the addict. This is indeed a heroic task since it involves a sizeable number of addicts belonging to deprived ethnic minority groups in New York City.

One of the thoughtless criticisms leveled at programs such as those carried on by Phoenix House is that addicts may function well while living and working within the treatment program and so long as they continue to participate in the follow-up activities of the program but that they relapse when "on their own" in society. This criticism overlooks the obvious fact that few (if any) individuals are ever on their own; that all of us are sustained and shaped through the support and association of our families, friends, and coworkers, indeed through the very existence of fortunate social and ecological arrangements. It is, however, precisely such social arrangements which have traditionally failed the drug addict and which reinforce and induce drug taking behavior. The addict left on his own has been returned to very malignant circumstances which reinforce a drug way of life.

How ironic it is that critics of programs such as Phoenix House overlook the fact that remission of addiction occurs among most of those who live and work at Phoenix House, that these victims of a supposed metabolic defect ably carry out socially responsible and often creative social and interpersonal activities without drugs when they are within a reconstructed social context which offers new associations, drug-free territories for human relationships and social efforts, and the opportunity to learn interactional and interpersonal skills.

The lessons from this kind of evidence seem clear. Any model for the treatment and rehabilitation of drug addicts must take into consideration how difficult it is for persons already on the drug route to "make it" in an addicting and drug pushing society, especially when they are limited by the many social and economic constraints forced upon them. Clearly, no program can succeed unless it is followed by new social arrangements, devised to provide human associations and territorial supports for the drug-free addict. Such programs though initially expensive will be far less costly to the community in the long run. In the final analysis the false model is always the more costly one.

The currently growing use of methadone for the treatment of heroin addiction is partly due to short-sighted economic considerations. Its enthusiasts can point to how inexpensive it is compared to comprehensive efforts to treat heroin addicts or to the costs of heroin addiction. The money issue here drowns out other, more relevant considerations. The irony is that the use of methadone to control the use of heroin substitutes one addiction for another. Despite some possible advantages to the use of methadone rather than heroin, we must not lose sight of the long-range consequences of addicting thousands of persons to a relatively unresearched drug whose long-term effects are still unknown. Opting for the popular solution exhibits the principle of least effort and succeeds only in deepening the prevailing mystification by perpetuating the drug means for the solution of human problems.

IX

The Prevention of Drug Misuse

In this book we have considered all drug giving and drug taking within one broad, general conceptual framework because we believe that the issues attaching to the use and abuse of legal drugs are similar to those attaching to the use and abuse of illicit drugs. We have not devoted special attention to the problem of alcohol precisely because we conceive of alcohol as only one among the many examples of drug misuse. The problems and the functions of alcohol are similar in many respects to those arising in the use of other drugs, and its use is similarly motivated.

Although most of the current voluminous writing about the misuse of drugs concerns the misuse of psychoactive agents by young people, and especially the use of drugs obtained illegally, it seems to us that to decry the use and misuse of drugs by young people while paying so little attention to the growing use and misuse of psychoactive agents in general, both those prescribed by physicians and those obtained over the counter without prescription, is highly misleading and unproductive.

A broader perspective gives rise to some conclusions about what social policies ought to be regarding the prevention of drug abuse which are very different from that implied by most of the discussions about psychoactive drugs in medical journals and the mass media. Such discussions tend to focus upon the individual as the target for intervention, rather than upon the larger problem of which the individual drug user is merely a symptom.

We view the problem of drug use and misuse as being located within a complex interlocking system that involves at least the drug industry, the medical profession, the mass media (including the underground press), and the user (whether he is a patient or a nonpatient). Recognition that the solution for the problem of drug abuse is somewhere among these interrelationships, then, demands imaginative social engineering rather than limited attention to one segment of the system with programs that appear to us to be merely patchwork remedies. It should now be clear that attention to the drug user himself represents only a small part of the solution to the problem of drug abuse.

Two analogies should clarify what steps in principle should be taken to implement programs for the prevention of drug abuse that have any reasonable probability of success. The first illustration concerns preventing accidents from taking place at a dangerous intersection. One approach to this problem, the traditional one, is to formulate an accident prevention program, including safety education, driver training and screening, warning signs, and traffic regulations requiring police enforcement (and incidentally adequate medical services to treat the victims). This illustration is analogous to current efforts to prevent drug abuse through educational campaigns aimed at potential drug users, through police and law enforcement and through medical and psychiatric treatment for the victims. A very different approach to the prevention of accidents at a dangerous intersection is to engineer the intersection out of existence, that is, to construct an overpass. We believe that efforts to prevent drug abuse must likewise deemphasize intervention at the level of the individual in favor of increasing efforts to modify the nature of the situation or the contexts that encourage drug use.

Consider also the example of the treatment of soldiers wounded in combat at any army field hospital. No amount of medical and surgical know-how, however successful at patching up wounded soldiers, will succeed in solving the larger problem, how to prevent soldiers from getting wounded. To do this one must bring an end to the war. In many respects, drug use, like war, is not a medical problem but a social, political, and economic one. Proceeding from this perspective, how might one go about changing the system of interlocking elements which contributes to the ever growing use and misuse of psychoactive drugs?

IMPLICATIONS FOR SOCIAL POLICY

In a technological era, in a society which has invested enormous resources in the invention and

100

marketing of chemicals and pharmaceuticals of all kinds and for all purposes, we can only be amused by the recommendation of Oliver Wendell Holmes that most drugs should be thrown "into the sea where it would be better for mankind and worse for the fishes." [1]

Drugs are a compelling fact of modern life, and new drugs will continue to be invented and used. Our purpose here is to outline a strategy which may lead to restrained use of psychoactive drugs by the medical profession and others, hopefully with clearly defined objectives in mind and with considerably less mystification than is currently implicit in their use. But the implementation of such a strategy is bound to fail unless changes are made in the whole system on a number of levels and at the same time.

We agree in principle with many of the suggestions and observations made by Richard Pillard [2] before Nelson's Congressional subcommittee. First, Pillard recommends that medical journals stop accepting drug advertisements completely or at the least greatly restrict the scope of such advertisements. Medical journals in turn will have to recognize the extent to which they are dependent on the pharmaceutical industry and will have to develop other sources of revenue including an appropriate subscription rate.

Second, we concur with Pillard's recom-

[1] *Medical Essays, 1842–1882* (Cambridge, Mass.: Riverside Press, 1891).
[2] Statement before the Subcommittee on Monopoly of the Select Committee on Small Business, July 30, 1969 (Washington, D.C.: Government Printing Office, 1969).

mendation that pharmaceutical houses "undertake a serious reconsideration of their promotional stategy, and reduce substantially the free distribution of drug samples to physicians." It is probably correct that many physicians "get into the habit of giving out sleeping pills and tranquilizers that come in the mail without the sort of serious thought that would go into writing a prescription."

The second target of our effort should be the medical profession, that is, the professional and social education of physicians. Physicians have engaged in the mystification of patients through psychoactive drugs for problems of everyday life, while at the same time being themselves victims of the cycle of mystification. A typical example of this process occurs when physicians prescribe sedating or mood-elevating drugs to older persons, even though it should be apparent that contemporary social arrangements lead to the physical isolation of the aged. In the November 16, 1970, San Francisco *Chronicle* appeared an Associated Press item entitled "Tranquilizers as Pacifiers":

> *The National Council of Senior Citzens accused the drug industry and doctors yesterday of promoting the use of tranquilizers in nursing homes for the sole purpose of quieting elderly patients. The council, urging a congressional investigation, said it has received an ever increasing number of complaints that patients who don't otherwise need the drugs are receiving them as pacifiers. Some doctors administer the drugs responsibly to emotionally disturbed patients, council president Nelson H. Cruik-*

*shank said, "but it appears that many doctors
. . . give blanket instructions to nursing home
staffs for use of tranquilizer drugs on patients
who do not need them. Exclusive use of tranquilizers can quickly reduce an ambulatory patient to a zombie, confining the patient to a
chair or bed, causing the patient's muscles to
atrophy from inaction, and causing general
health to deteriorate quickly," Cruikshank said
in a letter to Congressional leaders.*

Our prevailing age-discriminatory ideology, which
limits and devalues the participation of older persons in social systems, is the chief source of the unhappiness and misery experienced by older persons.

The discomfort, anxiety, or pain—however
one wishes to describe it—experienced by an unhap-
pily married woman, a salesman insecure in his work,
an adolescent caught between parental values and
those of his peer group can all be conceived of as
consequences of forces operating in the social context of which the individual or the patient is a member. Such social factors may consist of incompatible
demands made upon the individual, the guilt induced by not fulfilling expectations, or they may
consist of profoundly inadequate social arrangements.

The prescription of psychoactive drugs for
persons "victimized" in this way may permit them to
survive with less agony, to function, though with
some impairment, despite the disturbing social ar-
rangement. But an individually oriented "repair"
emphasis and the very act of defining the problems
as medical are dysfunctional for recognizing and un-

derstanding the role of the social determinants, and they detract from the attention required to alter social systems and the normative instructions prevailing within them.

Physicians should join with others in directing their efforts toward the creation of new social arrangements which will not exact an excessive toll in human suffering and unhappiness. Indeed, it may ultimately prove to be in his own best interests for a physician to reject the role of universal healer in favor of defining his area of competence and knowledgeability clearly to his prospective patients and to society at large. He should then follow this redefinition of the scope of his services by referring patients needing other resources to those agencies, organizations, and forces in society which are directly concerned with improving social systems, be they schools, the family, or the community.

While, in the long run, such referrals will be the most sensible solution, it does not seem to be a solution that can be put into operation in the immediate future. The medicalization of human problems in American life is already too deeply ingrained to be changed overnight. The present organization of social and health services which has been operative for some time reflects this mystification and will constrain tendencies toward change.

Since in all likelihood physicians will continue to serve a considerable number of persons who have been misdirected to seek their help and since drugs will continue to offer a quick and economical solution to the dilemma of being a physician with patients whose problems do not call for a physician, what constructive suggestions can be made? First, medical education regarding the action of psycho-active drugs should be strengthened considerably. Medical students must be exposed, early and repeatedly, to accurate information and to teachers who can influence them to exercise restraint with respect to the use of psychoactive agents despite pressures to the contrary.

Concomitant with a deemphasis of chemical solutions, medical education must be broadened to provide physicians with the training and skills to serve patients suffering from "humanitis" in other ways than through prescribing medication. This will not be a simple task. It will require educating physicians to view talking with and listening to patients as an integral element of the medical role. It will require teaching medical students to become skilled and practiced in the art of getting to know patients and to develop their curiosity beyond a patient's complaints to his family situation, his social situation, and his patterns of social relationships.

Present conditions of medical practice are such as to make it difficult for physicians to follow this new role model and conception. Physicians will have to familiarize themselves with the community, its strengths and vulnerabilities, and will have to know where to locate nonmedical resources to which patients may be referred for relief of distress. Also, the nonchemical treatment options involve interaction with patients and require efforts to comprehend difficult life situations. Providing such information and support to patients is a more time consuming procedure than the use of chemical options, but in the long run the exercise of options based on alternate models exacts far less in physiological, social, and psychological costs for the patient and the community at large.

We wish to make it clear that we are not advocating that physicians cease prescribing psychoactive drugs, but rather that they exercise restraint in doing so and give serious consideration to other options. The rationale for the administration of psychoactive drugs should proceed from a comprehensive model of human behavior rather than from the current symptom-disease medical model.

Since psychoactive drugs are already a fact of modern life, both prescribed drugs and those available without prescription (as well as illegal drugs) will continue to be manufactured, prescribed, marketed, and advertised. Psychoactive drugs, however, have exceedingly diffuse effects and immediate as well as long-range consequences, many of which are not visible for a considerable length of time after drug ingestion. Drugs affect a complex array of social, interactional, and psychological functions and have significant influences not only upon those who use the drugs but also upon all those with whom users come into intimate personal contact, especially their families, friends, and coworkers.

We have tried to emphasize in our discussion that psychoactive drugs are given and taken to achieve social and behavioral objectives. Their use to treat gross mental illness is relatively minor considered in the context of the whole spectrum of psychoactive drug use, unless one assumes that at any given time, one-third to one-half of the population are victims of "psychiatric illness." It is therefore no longer justifiable for physicians to limit their concern only to the effects of drugs on the symptoms of real or alleged mental illness or to focus upon too limited a segment of the consequences of drug use. Consequently, we urge physicians to join with social and behavioral scientists in a major effort to determine, for the first time, the broad range of consequences of psychoactive drug use and to define with as much precision as possible the ways in which the use of particular drugs effects and influences human behavior.

Proceeding from the comprehensive model of the role drugs play in human affairs generally presumes that physicians who prescribe drugs will become aware of the interpersonal and social effects produced by these psychoactive drugs, while at the same time retaining their traditional concern with physical side effects. Although there are at present tragically few objective data on these matters, it is well to remember Joel Elkes' [3] admonition that even a slight decrement in psychological functioning may have considerable behavioral repercussions. Thus, physicians must exercise both restraint and prudence in deciding to administer even a minor tranquilizer.

Drug maintenance as a long-term treatment strategy should probably be discontinued in all but a relatively small number of instances. We would include as possible candidates for long-term drug treatment only such severely disabled individuals who are not able to function adequately in interper-

[3] "Psychotropic Drugs: Observations on Current Views and Future Problems," in H. W. Brosin (Ed.), *Lectures on Experimental Psychiatry* (Pittsburgh: University of Pittsburgh Press, 1961), pp. 65–115.

sonal and work settings (even with drug treatment) but who nevertheless are less disturbed (and disturbing) when under the influence of such drugs as the phenothiazines. It should be borne in mind, however, that probably the effectiveness of drugs as a tool to produce behavioral change decreases over time. Drugs do seem to play an important role in short-term treatment of acute psychological disturbances but their use in long-term treatment does have severe physical consequences (tardive dyskinesia, for example) and diminishes interpersonal skills and behavior repertoires.

Drugs may be effective temporarily because they can produce overall changes in an individual's reactivity to anxiety, in his processing of information, and thereby in his relations with the significant persons surrounding him. They may assist in producing a temporary construction of an alternate mode of experiencing the world. This mode is desirable if an individual requires a moratorium in the sense of a temporary respite or a temporary boost or a temporarily altered sensory balance. These benefits of drugs rest to a considerable extent upon the kinds of figure-ground reversals they help to generate, that is, upon the changes in perception of what is important and what is relevant. But when drugs are used over an extended period of time, the alterations they produce tend to be assimilated and absorbed into the user's daily experiences and their effects become attenuated.

Social systems tend to readjust themselves so as to minimize the participation of drugged individuals. The individual himself experiences a dulling of psychological processes and a lack of motivation and skill to deal constructively with his changed status. Thus, the effectiveness of "drug therapy" hinges largely upon timing. Drug prescription must be anchored in a total treatment strategy with specific goals in mind. For example, a sleeping pill is useful if an individual is temporarily overwhelmed by problems and cannot sleep, but its use should be discontinued when the crisis is passed. Similarly a drug may be useful for the duration of an unpleasant airplane ride but dysfunctional when administered on a regular basis to make individuals able to withstand the unpleasantness of a distasteful job or work situation.

Stimulant drugs, for example, have been and no doubt will continue to be used for an occasional "heroic" effort such as that of a composer struggling against a deadline to complete a score for a show about to open. But if stimulant drugs are employed to maintain a level of performance which continuously overtaxes an individual's capacity, their effects soon become physiologically and socially dysfunctional. In general, we see psychoactive drugs as useful tools in the management of short-term and severe crises when there is insufficient time to mobilize other resources and evolve appropriate human arrangements to assist an individual. However, drugs should not be routinely employed in the management of troubled and troublesome persons. Such use in the long run damages the ability of the individual and others, whether family members or hospital staff, to relate to each other when the chemical medium is withdrawn.

Mystification and Drug Misuse

Like the general public, educators, teachers, and school administrators have restricted their attention to only a small part of the drug misuse problem. By neglecting the larger problem of drug use and the interlocking complex of factors that tend to induct young and old alike into a way of life in which drug solutions are sought for human problems and dilemmas, educators contribute to the problem while manifestly being deeply concerned with its solution.

Many school systems cooperate in the widespread administration of psychoactive drugs to school children. In Omaha, as mentioned earlier, between 5 and 10 per cent of the 62,000 school children were given behavior modification drugs to make them less hyperactive and more manageable. The intensive use of these drugs in the Omaha school system has been described as "being part of a national pattern for coping with *hyperactive* children" (our italics). "Sometimes children get so restless they fall off their chairs in class," a school nurse in New York comments.[4] At the same time some parents are "dosing their children with tranquilizers before sending them off to school," according to Geoffrey Esty,[5] a pediatrician assigned to the New Jersey State Education Department. Some parents do this in order to "protect the children from cracking under pressure. . . . I have since found out from fellow pediatricians," says Esty, "that parents

[4] *San Francisco Chronicle,* July 2, 1970.
[5] *New York Post,* May 25, 1964.

110

are slipping the children sedatives, too. They tell me it is quite common." Teachers who have trouble with a particular child often request the parent to get a prescription for the child from the family physician. In so doing, teachers then become an integral part of the cycle of mystification. They too are persuaded that human discomfort and distress are to be managed chemically. They consider a child who is restless, tense, and who cannot sit still in presently arranged educational contexts as disturbed and as a proper target for chemical management.

It is likewise ironical that the renewed sensitivity of medical and mental health workers to human suffering and other humanitarian concerns has been reflected primarily in their substitution of chemical restraints for mechanical ones. Since the chemical response serves, often unwittingly, to perpetuate malignant social arrangements, the change is perhaps more apparent than real. We are reminded of the observation that after the advent of psychoactive drugs, mental hospitals "looked so much better." Nursing homes too in which the residents are drugged may present a good and pleasing appearance, but the external appearance belies the significant fact that the quality of life in nursing homes is not necessarily improved by the drugs.

Amphetamines have been used with some success in reducing gross hyperactivity in samples of severely disturbed and institutionalized youngsters.[6] This finding has been exploited to persuade some physicians and educators to use drugs to make

[6] C. Bradley, "Benzedrine and Dexedrine in the Treatment of Children's Behavior Disorders," *Pediatrics,* 1950, *5*, 24–38.

ordinary youngsters more tractable by drugging them en masse.

It would be far more sensible to improve school systems and to make them into appropriate learning environments than to drug youngsters who are bored or distressed by inadequate learning situations. Here is another clear example of how psychoactive drugs are used as alternatives to making constructive changes in the pattern of social arrangements and how segments of society become unwitting collaborators in opting for chemical solutions.

Teachers and administrators of education systems thus become agents in the induction of young people into drug taking as a mode for solving problems and employ drugs themselves to solve their own problems (such as large classes, poor training, and inadequate resources). These same teachers, administrators, and education officials are then appalled by the widespread incidence of illegal drug use among their charges. Their inability to see the connection between the two sides of the coin and to see that they as well as the young people are victims of the same kind of mystification is ironical.

Drug education for teachers makes sense only if it is conducted with the objective of demystification and from a perspective which places the giving and taking of drugs, whether prescribed or self-administered, within the same conceptual framework. Teachers and administrators need to be sensitized to the forces that promulgate chemical options to youth and society at large, whether these be the medical profession, the media, or the youth culture.

The metaphor of the machine runs deep in our culture. Physicians and hippies alike tend to treat the body as if it were a machine and, paradoxically, to seek meaning through chemicals as well. Both are truly members of the same technological culture and both are enveloped by the same demand for rapid change. As Philip Slater says in *The Pursuit of Loneliness:*

> *If the body can be used as a working machine and a consuming machine, why not an experience machine? The drug user makes precisely the same assumption as do other Americans— that the body is some sort of appliance. Hence they must "turn on" and "tune in" in their unsuccessful effort to drop out. They may be enjoying the current more, but they are still plugged into the same machinery that drives other Americans on their weary and joyless round.*[7]

Norman Mailer sees the change taking place even in the group of men presumably interested in humanistic pursuits, the psychoanalysts: "People in analysis began to be subjected to men who were no longer cultivated, poetic, deep, and engaged in intellectual activity, but to men who were technicians, essentially interested in dominating the material before them, treating them as a commodity, as a machine to be successfully redesigned."[8] The logical extension of the enterprise of such "technicians" is to develop and utilize tools. Drugs are tools that are

[7] *The Pursuit of Loneliness: American Culture at the Breaking Point* (Boston: Beacon, 1970), p. 93.
[8] Quoted in the *New York Times,* August 4, 1968, p. 58.

introduced into the human "machines" to make them better and to make them run smoothly.

If our argument is essentially correct and drugs do serve as substitutes for human relatedness and experience, then the problem for an educator becomes how to displace the use of drugs with human relationships and with social contexts which generate rich and varied inner experiences in young people. As Harley Shands [9] has so beautifully formulated it, complete socialization—learning the complexities of becoming human—occurs only within the context of a human relationship. Educational systems, as currently constituted, unfortunately do not often provide such contexts. All too often, the structure of a school or a university destroys the connection between knowledge and the human context out of which it derives and to which it must ultimately be related.

All kinds of learning are facilitated, indeed can only occur, within the context of human relationships. Human beings initially achieve their sense of self and the ability to interact with others through being participants in close relationships with other human beings. The acquisition of information and the learning of skills—artistic and technical—have traditionally occurred within the context of a personal relationship between master and apprentice, teacher and student. McLuhan is probably correct in saying that television has become the single most important teacher and informational input to the young, but television, like teaching machines, audio-

[9] *The War with Words: Communication and Consciousness* (The Hague: Mouton Press, in press).

visual aids, and canned lectures, provides information outside the context of human relatedness.

Moreover, the constraints operating in most elementary schools and high schools frequently do not make relationships between teachers and students possible. Teachers often see their job as one of communicating information and skills in their subject matter and maintaining order and discipline in the classroom, not as one involved in the creation of relationship paradigms. Many educators, from elementary school teachers to university professors, are so caught up in the contemporary technological ethos that they do not view themselves as involved in personal relationships with students and do not view themselves as interactional mentors and guides. Only too often education occurs within a climate of objectivity without exhilaration and excitement and without the creation of sensory and visceral experiences.

Lacking a climate of relatedness, spending most of their time within social contexts which are devoid of excitement and which are unproductive of inner experience, young people are driven to seek affects in drugs. Harry Wilmer,[10] director of an innovative youth drug ward at the University of California, says of his patients that they "take drugs because . . . they want to feel. . . . They relate mechanically, without love, excitement, and rewarding feelings. . . . Bad feelings seem preferable to them to no feelings."

The dilemma is that drugs provide only ef-

[10] *Children of Sham* (in preparation).

fects, no learning, and it is learning and exercising of the means of obtaining such effects that constitute a vital part of human life and provide the substance and repetitive structures of human activity and experience. If they learn from machines, if they watch television (a medium that advertises participation but neither permits nor teaches the means to achieve it), if they are exposed only to the myth of objectivity and sit in classes and lecture halls stripped of human inputs, where are young people to learn how to be human? How shall they become more than mere servomechanisms of the multiple technologies which envelop them?

We address our recommendations to educators who are deeply committed to young people, who are concerned with the use and abuse of drugs, and who search for a position from which to direct their efforts. We urge them to eschew the traditional tunnel-vision approach to the problem, such as is implied by special programs of drug education and the hiring of persons with alleged special expertise in the drug problems of the young. These, in our view, only further perpetuate the mystification of the problem. Such programs imply that the taking of drugs is the problem, while, in fact, social arrangements, not merely drugs, generate drug use, and many segments of society collaborate in misrepresenting drugs as solutions.

The attention of educators must be directed to the quality of the human interaction and relatedness which occur within their orbit. They must come to grips with the not inconsiderable task of restructuring educational contexts in such a way that meaningful human contact between students, and especially between teachers and students, is facilitated. To achieve this restructuring requires territorial transformations to provide settings and places which encourage and generate differentiated human interaction. It may demand the educators' support of rather than antagonism to new social arrangements which have spontaneously evolved among students. Living arrangements such as communes should be understood as experiments, albeit often unsuccessful ones, in establishing human relatedness.

Unless educational contexts can be peopled with those who conceive of themselves in a new way, the outlook for turning students on to human relationships rather than to drugs will remain bleak. Even were more persons who are concerned with human relationships brought into educational contexts, the outlook for generating involvement and excitement within our current educational framework is not promising. However, in the community are many social contexts in which participants can experience a high degree of excitement and involvement. And some of these are staffed by persons who, though not professional educators, would enjoy being related to young people as preceptors, guides, and teachers.

What we are trying to suggest is an effort to link persons who derive excitement and joy from human interaction (and who are willing to share this excitement) with young persons looking for something or someone to relate to. Learning within such contexts seems to us to be infinitely preferable to the suggestion that education in the future be accomplished through the ingestion of learning pills.

Perhaps it would be wiser to reject the drug

117

route altogether as a long-range solution to the human and social problems that beset modern man. Our critics argue that drugs fill a need, given the present constraints upon changing prevailing social arrangements in schools, hospitals, nursing homes, indeed, in the society at large; for now, they say, drugs represent the best and perhaps the only answer. To accept such pseudosolutions, however, is often tantamount to accepting them as final ones. Once we are convinced they work, even in the short run, even temporarily, we tend to embrace them. Acceptance then amputates the search for alternatives.

Any solution once adopted tends to establish a self-perpetuating system. If the drug solution did not exist, we would be forced to pursue alternatives more vigorously. Since it does exist, we are not forced to seek alternatives but must do so voluntarily and against the resistance of those who support that which is already familiar. Hence, those who seek more comprehensive and new alternatives and more humane solutions must speak especially loud to be heard.

Drug giving and drug taking represent all too brittle and undiscriminating responses to human problems, and ultimately, in our view, they breed only frustration and alienation. Changing the human environment is a monumental undertaking. Seeking to change cognitive shapes through chemical means may appear to be convenient and economical, but the drug solution is already rapidly becoming another technological Trojan Horse.

Bibliography

American Journal of Diseases of Children, 1969, *118* (2).

APPLETON, W. S. "Snow Phenomenon." *Psychiatry,* 1965, *28,* 88–93.

BALTER, M. Address given to the American Public Health Association, Houston, October 1970.

BARBER, B. *Drugs and Society.* New York: Russell Sage Foundation, 1967.

BECKER, H. S. "History, Culture and Subjective Experience: An Exploration of the Social Bases of Drug-Induced Experiences." *Journal of Health and Social Behavior,* 1967, *8* (3), 163–176.

BEECHER, H. K. *Measurement of Subjective Responses, Quantitative Affects of Drugs.* New York: Oxford University Press, 1959.

BLUM, R. H., and associates. *Students and Drugs.* San Francisco: Jossey-Bass, 1969.

BRODKIN, H. Testimony before the Subcommittee on Monopoly of the Select Committee on Small Business, July 1969. Washington, D.C.: Government Printing Office, 1969.

CHEIN, I. "Psychological Functions of Drug Use." In H. Steinberg (Ed.), *Scientific Basis of Drug Dependence, A Symposium.* London: J & A Churchill, 1969.

CLAUSEN, J. "Drug Addiction." In R. K. Merton and R. A. Nisbet (Eds.), *Contemporary Social Problems.* New York: Harcourt Brace Jovanovich, 1967.

CORRY, J. "The Politics of Style," *Harper's Magazine*, 1970, *241* (1446).

CRANE, G. E. AND GARDNER, R., JR., (Eds.) *Psychotropic Drugs and Dysfunctions of the Basal Ganglia: A Multidisciplinary Workshop.* Public Health Service Publication, No. 1938. Washington, D.C.: Government Printing Office, 1969.

CURIE, E. *Madame Curie.* New York: Doubleday, 1938.

DUBOIS, R. "On the Present Limitation of Drug Research." In P. Talalay (Ed.), *Drugs in our Society.* Baltimore: Johns Hopkins University Press, 1964.

EHRLICH, P. Address delivered at the dedication of the Georg-Speyer-Haus, September 1906. In F. Himmelwert (Ed.), *The Collected Papers of Paul Ehrlich*, Vol. 3. London: Pergamon, 1960.

FREUD, E. L. *The Letters of Sigmund Freud.* New York: McGraw-Hill, 1960.

FRIEDMAN, D. X. Testimony before the Subcommittee on Monopoly of the Select Committee on Small Business, July 1969. Washington, D.C.: Government Printing Office, 1969.

GARAI, P. Quoted in S. Malitz, "Psychopharmacology: A Cultural Approach." In *Symposium: Non-Narcotic Drug Dependency and Addiction,* proceedings of the New York County District Branch, American Psychiatric Association, March 1966.

GROSS, L. "The Tragedy of Thalidomide Babies: Preview of a German Horror Trial." *Look,* May 28, 1968.

HAYMAN, M., AND DITMAN, R. "Influence of Age and Orientation of Psychiatrists on Their Use of Drugs." *Comprehensive Psychiatry*, 1966, 7, 152–165.

HORDERN, A. In C. R. B. Joyce (Ed.), *Psychopharmacology.* Philadelphia: Lippincott, 1968.

HOWARD, J. *Please Touch.* New York: McGraw-Hill, 1970.

IMSENG, V. "Erstbesteigung des Sudlenz." In SAAS-FE Information 1970/1971. Buchdruckerei, Visp A6.

Bibliography

JONES, E. *The Life and Work of Sigmund Freud.* New York: Basic Books, 1957.

JONES, R. T. "Marijuana Myths," unpublished manuscript, Langley Porter Neuropsychiatric Institute, San Francisco, 1970.

Journal of the American College Health Association, 1969, *17* (5).

KLERMAN, G. L., SHARAF, M. R., HOLZMAN, M., AND LEVINSON, D. J. "Sociopsychological Characteristics of Resident Psychiatrists and Their Use of Drug Therapy." *American Journal of Psychiatry,* 1960, *117.*

KESEY, K. Quoted in T. Wolfe, *The Electric Kool-Aide Acid Test.* New York: Farrar, Straus and Giroux, 1968.

LABORIT, H., AND HUEGENARD, P. *Journal of Chir.,* 1951, *67* (631).

LENNARD, H. L. *A Proposed Program of Research in Socio-pharmacology.* In P. H. Leiderman and D. Shapiro (Eds.), *Psychobiological Approaches to Social Behavior.* Palo Alto, Calif.: Stanford University Press, 1964, pp. 127–137.

LENNARD, H. L., AND BERNSTEIN, A. *Patterns in Human Interaction: An Introduction to Clinical Sociology.* San Francisco: Jossey-Bass, 1969.

LENNARD, H. L., EPSTEIN, L. J., BERNSTEIN, A., AND RANSOM, D. C. *Drug Giving and Drug Taking: An Introduction to Sociopharmacology.* Chicago: University of Chicago Press. In preparation.

LENNARD, H. L., EPSTEIN, L. J., BERNSTEIN, A., AND RANSOM, D. C. "Hazards Implicit in Prescribing Psychoactive Drugs," *Science,* 1970, *169,* 438–441.

LENNARD, H. L., EPSTEIN, L. J., AND KATZUNG, B. G. "Psychoactive Drug Action and Group Interaction Process." *Journal of Nervous and Mental Disease,* 1967, *145,* 69–78.

MALITZ, S. "Psychopharmacology: A Cultural Approach."

Mystification and Drug Misuse

In *Symposium: Non-Narcotic Drug Dependency and Addiction.* Proceedings of the New York County District Branch, American Psychological Association, March 1966.

MC LUHAN, M. *Understanding Media: The Extensions of Man.* New York: McGraw-Hill, 1964.

MARTIN, W. "Preferences for Types of Patients." In R. K. Merton, G. Reader, and P. L. Kendall (Eds.), *The Student Physician.* Cambridge, Mass.: Harvard University Press, 1957.

Medical Newsletter, 1969, *11* (20).

MENDEL, W. "Tranquilizer Prescribing as a Function of the Experience and Ability of the Therapist." *American Journal of Psychiatry*, 1967, *124*.

MERTON, R. K. *Social Theory and Social Structure* (Rev. Ed.). New York: The Free Press, 1957.

NELSON, G. Opening Statement before the Subcommittee on Monopoly of the Select Committee on Small Business, July 1969. Washington, D.C.: Government Printing Office, 1969.

NOWLIS, V., AND NOWLIS, H. H. "The Description and Analysis of Mood." *Annals of the New York Academy of Science*, 1956, *65*, 345–355.

PARRY, H. J. "Use of Psychotropic Drugs by U.S. Adults." Public Health Reports, 1968, *83* (10).

PILLARD, R. C. Statement before the Subcommittee on Monopoly of the Select Committee on Small Business, July 1969. Washington, D.C.: Government Printing Office, 1969.

RABKIN, R. *Inner and Outer Space.* New York: Norton, 1970.

ROSZAK, T. *The Making of a Counter Culture.* Garden City, N.Y.: Doubleday, 1969.

San Francisco Chronicle, June 29, 1970.

SCHACHTER, S. "Interaction of Cognitive and Physiological Determinants of Emotional States," paper given at Symposium on Psychological Approaches to Human

Behavior, Harvard Medical School, Cambridge, Mass., April 1963.

SCHACHTER, S. In P. H. Leiderman and D. Shapiro (Eds.), *Psychobiological Approaches to Social Behavior.* Palo Alto, Calif.: Stanford University Press, 1964, pp. 138–173.

SHABSHIN, M., AND EISEN, M. B. "Effects of Ward Tension on the Quality and Quantity of Tranquilizer Utilization." *Annals of the New York Academy of Science,* 1957, *67,* 746–757.

SINCLAIR, W. J. *Semmelweis, His Life and Doctrine.* Manchester at the University Press, 1909.

STARKWEATHER, J. A. "Individual and Situational Influences on Drug Effects." In R. M. Featherstone and A. Simon (Eds.), *Psychopharmacology.* Springfield: Thomas, 1959.

WILSON, C. M., AND HUBY, P. "An Assessment of the Responses to Drugs Acting on the Central Nervous System," *Clinical Pharmocology and Therapeutics,* 2, (5), 587–598.

WITTEN, C. Address given by President-Elect to the American Academy of General Practice. In *Symposium: Non-Narcotic Drug Dependency and Addiction,* proceedings of the New York County District Branch, American Psychological Association, March 1966.

Acknowledgements

The ideas presented in this book are a result of genuine collaboration. We discussed, debated, and argued among ourselves until we reached formulations which were acceptable to each of us.

Over the years we received encouragement and stimulation from many colleagues and friends. It was Murray E. Jarvik and Harold Abramson who first interested one of us in the study of drugs and social behavior. We were fortunate to meet Bertram Katzung and Frederick Myers, pharmacologists at the San Francisco Medical Center, and psychopharmacologist Hannah Steinberg, at the University of London Medical School, who shared our convictions that research on psychoactive drugs and their effects should not be the exclusive prerogative of any one discipline or professional group. Robert K. Merton and Joel Elkes, outstanding representatives of sociology and clinical psychiatry, respectively, urged the senior author to pursue his interest in sociopharmacology.

Hilde Bruch, Theodore Sarbin, Stanley Schachter, and Harley Shands profoundly influenced our thinking on the relation between social-symbolic and physiological processes. Our debt to their formulations is considerable.

Howard Becker, Norman Bell, Robert Brissenden, Herbert Leiderman, Al Siegel, John Weakland, and Ken Willinger devoted many hours to exploring with us the

124

Acknowledgements

issues discussed in this book, and their comments have been most stimulating. Sidney Malitz, a pioneer of psychiatric drug research, read the entire manuscript and made many helpful suggestions. Nathan Kline over the years has tried to broaden the scope of research on psychoactive drugs. We remember with gratitude his encouragement of social and behavioral scientists to work in this area. We are also grateful to Orville Brim, Jr., president of the Russell Sage Foundation for providing support for a Conference on Training and Research in Sociopharmacology at a critical juncture in our efforts.

Senator Gaylord Nelson, his administrative staff, and members of his Subcommittee have for years provided a public forum for an intelligent exposition of the social forces responsible for increased drug use and misuse in our society. The transcripts of the hearings of the Nelson Committee have been most helpful in our work. We want to express our high regard for the impressive efforts of Senator Nelson, his staff, and his committee.

Finally, our deep appreciation goes to Alexander Simon, chairman of the Department of Psychiatry at the San Francisco Medical Center, University of California, for creating an intellectual climate in which investigators carry out research freely and are encouraged to develop their own position on controversial issues without interference or censorship.

Biographical Notes

HENRY L. LENNARD is associate professor of medical sociology in the Department of Psychiatry at the San Francisco Medical Center of the University of California. He lectures in the Department of Sociology at Berkeley, and is a NIMH Research Career Scientist at the Langley Porter Neuropsychiatric Institute in San Francisco, where he directs the Family Study Station. He was one of the first social scientists to research and write about the effects of psychoactive drugs on social behavior and to define the parameters of sociopharmacology. Previously Lennard was codirector of the Mental Health Training and Research Program in the Department of Sociology and the Bureau of Applied Social Research at Columbia University, and also served on the Graduate Faculties of the New School and the University of Colorado. He has also been a consultant to the Cold Spring Harbor Biological Laboratories and to the Departments of Psychiatry of the Downstate Medical Center, State University of New York and of Roosevelt Hospital. Lennard received the Ph.D. degree from Columbia in 1955. He is coauthor with Arnold Bernstein of *The Anatomy of Psychotherapy*, Columbia University Press, 1960, and *Patterns in Human Interaction: An Introduction to Clinical Sociology*, Jossey-Bass Publishers, 1969.

LEON J. EPSTEIN is professor of psychiatry at the San Francisco Medical Center of the University of California, and Associate Medical Director of the Langley Porter Neuropsychiatric Institute. He is a fellow of the American Psychiatric Association, and served as chairman of its Committee on Research. Epstein has been involved in a number of studies on the effect of psychoactive drugs and their relationship to Hospital Release Rates, and more recently has collaborated with Lennard on studies of the effect of psychoactive drugs on group processes. He has also been involved in studies of geriatric psychiatry. Formerly, Epstein held the position of deputy director of research at the California State Department of Mental Hygiene. He received a Ph.D. in psychology from Peabody College in 1941, and his M.D. from the University of Tennessee Medical School in 1949. He is the coauthor, with Alexander Simon and Marjorie Fiske Lowenthal, of *Crisis and Intervention,* published by Jossey-Bass, 1970.

ARNOLD BERNSTEIN is professor of psychology at Queens College of the City University of New York. He is research consultant to the Department of Psychiatry at the Metropolitan Hospital Center of New York Medical College and to the Langley Porter Neuropsychiatric Institute. He is also in private practice in New York City. He was one of the original members of the board of directors of Narcotics Anonymous. He has also served on the faculties of Teachers College, Columbia University, and of the City College of New York. He is a former president of the Council of Psychoanalytic Psychotherapists, and the former chief of the Psychological Clinic at Stuyvesant Polyclinic Hospital. Bernstein received the Ph.D. from Columbia University in 1952.

DONALD C. RANSOM is an assistant professor in the Division of Ambulatory and Community Medicine at the San Francisco Medical Center of the University of California. He is research coordinator at the Family Study Station, Langley

Porter Neuropsychiatric Institute, and is a consultant to both the Alcoholism Program of San Joaquin County Medical Facilities and the Personnel Division of the Bank of California. Ransom received a B.A. degree in social relations from Harvard (1965), an M.A. degree in sociology from the University of California, Berkeley (1966), and a Ph.D. degree in clinical psychology also from Berkeley (1970).

STEVEN D. ALLEN is currently a research associate at the Family Study Station, Langley Porter Neuropsychiatric Institute. He is a consultant to the Alcoholism Program of San Joaquin County Medical Facilities. He has worked as a psychotherapist and program consultant in the Adolescent Drug Abuse Treatment Program at Mendocino State Hospital, Talmage, California. Allen received a B.S. degree in psychology from the University of Ilinois in 1964. He is at present a doctoral candidate in clinical psychology at the University of California, Berkeley.

Index

Index

Drug companies. *See* Pharmaceutical industry
Drug effects, 75; on behavior and experience, 57–58; context of, 63–66; diffusion of, 81–82, 85–86; drug user as judge of, 5, 14, 58–66; misjudgments about, 62–66; models of, 80, 82–83; myths about, 59, 61, 66; as socially learned, 57, 60. *See also* Side effects
Drug giving: benefits to physicians of, 25–28; characteristics of prescriptions and, 32–34; hidden functions of, 25–26; variations in, 28–37
Drug taking, consequences of, 1, 3, 14, 46, 54–56, 67–76; on emotions, 71–72; as extension of biochemistry, 68–69; on family function, 30, 53, 76, 86–88; hidden, 68–70, 75; on human group, 69, 71–72; in mental patients, 73–74, 85; for self-regulation mechanism, 70–71
Drug therapy: and crisis management, 109; model for, 107–109
Drugs, psychoactive: history of, 80; increase of sale of, 17, 23; knowledge about, 2, 12–13; as new technology, 68–69, 74–75; as perpetuating social ills, 25, 118; properties of, 47–48, 52–55; reasons for using, 45–51; research needed on,

Drugs *(Cont.)*:
12–13, 76; types of, 10
DUBOS, R., 79

E

Ecological model, 13
Education, drug prevention in, 110–117
Effects. *See* Drug effects
EHRLICH, P., 78
EISEN, M. B., 29
Elavil, 78
ELKES, J., 107
Emotional states: structure of, 82–84; treatment of, 19–21, 71–72
Encounter groups, 52
Energizers, 10
Enzyme systems, 73
ESTY, G., 110

F

Family, effect of drug use on, 30, 53, 76, 86–88
FAULKNER, J., 40
Federal Trade Commission, 17
FREEDMAN, D. X., 72
FREUD, S., 3–5

G

GARAI, P., 16
Geigy Pharmaceutical, 21

H

Hallucinogenic drugs, 6, 8, 27, 52, 55, 59, 76
HALSTEAD, W. W., 7
Heroin, 11, 89–90, 96

Index

Index

S

SCHACHTER, S., 64n, 82–83
Schizophrenia, 35
Schools and drugs, 31–32, 110–117
Sedatives, 1, 5, 10, 31, 72, 84, 111
Self-mystification, 46–47
SEMMELWEIS, I. P., 77
Sensitivity training, 52
Sensory modalities, 52
Sex, drug prescription by, 36
SHABSIN, M., 29
SHANDS, H., 114
Side effects of drugs: cost of, 2–3, 5, 12, 14, 25, 67–68, 72–74, 79–81; definition of, 79–80
SINCLAIR, SIR W. J., 76–77
SLATER, P., 113
Social characteristics and drug use, 33, 36
Social effects of drug use, 12–13, 25, 47–56, 69, 71–72, 81, 85–87, 89–94, 103–104, 108
Socialization, 114
Spanish fly, 84
Speed freak, 12
STARKWEATHER, J. A., 86
Stimulants, 59, 61, 76, 109
STRAUSS, A., 37
Subcommittee on Monopoly of the Select Committee on Small Business, 22n, 40n, 72n, 101

T

Tardive dyskinesia, 73–74, 108
Teachers, drug education for, 112
Television, 49–50, 114–116

Thalidomide, 69–70
THC, 60
Therapists, nonmedical, 33
THOMAS, W. I., 27
Tofranil, 21–22, 31
Toxicity, 80
Treatment of drug misuse, 88–91; individual focus of, 88–91; programs for, 91–96
Tranquilizers, 1, 6, 9–10, 16, 22, 26, 36, 61, 76, 84, 102–103, 110
"Turned on," 53–54

U

U.S. Food and Drug Administration, 32
Uppers, 65
User and judge of drug effects, 5, 14, 58–66

V

Values, questions of, 6, 54–55
Valium, 33, 84
Vistaril, 20

W

WILMER, H., 115
WILSON, C. M., 61, 65
WOLFE, T., 55

X

X rays, 7

Y

Youth culture, 3, 11, 14, 27, 45–55

DATE DUE

FEB 1 2 76			
MAR 1 6 76			
NOV 18 76			
DEC 8 77			
APR 5 1979			
NOV 6 1980			
NOV 2 7 1980			
APR 1 2 1984			
APR 1 1 1985			
DEC 1 2 1985			
DEC 1 8 1986			
APR 1 2 1989			
APR 1 0 1990			
NOV 2 1 1996			